JUST CALL ME BILLY

PHOTOGRAPH BY CHARLES NICHOLAS / *THE COMMERCIAL APPEAL* / LANDOV

JUST CALL ME BILLY

THE LIFE AND TIMES OF BILLY DUNAVANT

WITH RON HIGGINS

FOREWORD BY FREDERICK W. SMITH

FIRST AMERICAN EDITION
ISBN 978-099687790-9

CONTEMPORARY MEDIA, INC. | 460 TENNESSEE STREET, SUITE 200 | MEMPHIS, TENNESSEE 38103

Contents

Tommie Dunavant or, in Billy's words, "Pretty Legs."

Dedication

I know I'm a George Strait man, but there's other country music that hits home with me as well.

When I think about this dedication, I am reminded of Kenny Rogers' song, "Through the Years," especially the lyric, "For through the years you have never let me down."

Through the process of writing this book, you have never let me down.

You have been there from start to finish, tirelessly working and constantly encouraging me.

So I dedicate this book to my one and only, my beautiful wife Tommie.

Because with her, I can't "imagine anything the two of us can't do."

Billy

Frederick W. Smith, Chairman and CEO of FedEx Corporation.

Foreword

I'VE KNOWN BILLY DUNAVANT FOR A VERY LONG TIME in various ways. Perhaps the most public was in his role as the potential lead owner of an investment group, of which I was part, to get one of two NFL expansion franchises for Memphis in the early 1990s.

Also, Billy's wife, Tommie, is my second cousin's widow. But I've known Billy the longest through many civic and charitable endeavors we've been involved in through the years.

Memphis has about a dozen people and institutions that "carry the load" for any kind of major community or philanthropic project. The names have changed slightly over the years because of age, but there have always been only a few you can count on to step up. Billy was always at the top of the list.

Without exception, he was someone who would weigh in and help if you needed funding for, say, the Boy Scouts, the Boys and Girls Clubs, a University of Memphis project. There was never a long gestation period with Billy, which was an admirable and appreciated trait. You got a quick "yes" and always a generous contribution. I don't think he ever declined a request. Everybody who knows Billy well is familiar with his generosity and willingness to support so many worthwhile causes. He's a very kind and generous man, especially to those in need.

I've always respected Billy as a businessman. He reached the pinnacle of the cotton business because of his unmatched and detailed understanding of this huge worldwide market. Billy can synthesize an enormous amount of disparate information

"If you've ever watched Billy play tennis you know he wasn't out there just punching the ball." — Fred Smith

such as the weather in India, a boll weevil outbreak in Mississippi, floods in Egypt, fashion trends, and obscure political events that influence the global cotton trade.

If you've ever watched Billy play tennis you know he wasn't out there just punching the ball. He was out there to beat the stew out of his opponent. He *loves* competition. He showed that when he owned the Showboats, Memphis' USFL franchise in the 1980s, and Billy applied that same competitiveness to his business.

Playing in such a dynamic fast-paced market, Billy found the ultimate game – it was like tennis or football on steroids. I always thought he felt the cotton market came as close as one could to playing a game at the highest level of business.

Billy has a great sense of humor. He's often very funny, constantly making fun of things – especially himself! He's fun to be around, and his wit and incisive conversation make spending time with him an enjoyable experience.

I regret that his enormous contributions to Memphis probably are not well known to the average person, perhaps because his business didn't have a brand name like FedEx or AutoZone or Holiday Inn. Yet what Billy has done for the city and everyone who lives here is certainly known to the people who are involved with many charities and major civic endeavors.

Billy Dunavant is a great gentleman; a business legend known for his integrity and hard work; and a generous philanthropist who has helped countless people – many who will never hear his name. He's a really good guy whom I respect and admire, and I've been proud to count him as a friend for many years.

I'm glad he's finally telling his remarkable story.

Frederick W. Smith
Founder, Chairman, and CEO
FedEx Corporation

Hall-of-Famer Reggie White lifts Billy off the ground celebrating a Showboats touchdown. Reggie played for Billy in 1984 and 1985 and they remained close personal friends until his untimely death in 2004.

Introduction

My life's been grand,
I've been a hand at livin' it up all the way,
I've had good times and bad times,
And hard times and done time,
Life's been a blessing every day.

I WISH I COULD CLAIM I WROTE THOSE SONG LYRICS, but they were written by Merle Haggard and a co-writer, and sung by George Strait, my favorite singer.

As I wrote this book with Ron Higgins, looking back at what I've done, where I've been and who has touched my life, I felt like old George was singing about me.

Which is why George makes several "guest" appearances throughout this book that people closest to me suggested over the last years I should write after I officially retired.

My answer every time was, "Why do I want a book about ME?"

My wife Tommie unsuccessfully tried four or five years ago to get me to write a book. She was smart enough to let it rest for a long time before making another run at me. When I finally agreed, she got all excited.

The easiest thing was coming up with the book title.

I've never liked being called "William" or "Mr. Dunavant." Now, "Mr. D." or "Boss" or "Bossman" works just fine.

But whether you're a president of a country or a farmhand and you address me as Mr. Dunavant, the first thing I'm going to say to you is, "Just call me Billy."

So there you go.

I'd never taken the time ever to stand back and look at my life and my career. I just kept going full speed ahead.

There's no time to reflect in the cotton business. If you do that, you're probably getting your butt beat by your competitors.

Every day was a new day to me. When the clock struck midnight, it didn't matter what you did the day before, good or bad.

Each day held fresh challenges, but that's why I loved what I did. It was rarely the same, day-to-day, even hour-to-hour.

I got the most out of each day. I didn't leave anything unturned. But when the day was over, it was over.

Now did I do things after hours? Aw hell yeah, every night. But I was in control. I could handle that.

I thrived on the fast daily pace, so I never slowed down long enough to put everything in perspective.

Writing a book wasn't as painful as I thought it was going to be. In fact, all the reflecting made me realize how good my life has been. I guess I've accomplished a lot, but one of the great things about looking back is realizing all the friends I've made and the relationships I've established.

There are a lot of relationships, but that's one reason I had a successful business career. It's all about the relationships you make and maintain.

I know I've touched a lot of people as I've walked through life, but just as many people or more have touched me. When I make friends or they make friends with me, we always stay close. I don't regret any of my friendships.

It's been a hard day's night. One of Billy's many loving pets looks on as his master takes a well-deserved rest.

Maybe one reason I wrote this book is to acknowledge how much I've appreciated all the people I've connected with through the years, including the loyal employees who helped Dunavant Enterprises become a worldwide name in the cotton business.

I guess this book wasn't a bad idea after all. I've loved looking back on my life and career. Like George Strait sings, my life has been a blessing every day.

At age 16, Billy won the top skeet shooting title at the Hatchie Coon Hunting and Fishing Club in Tulot, Arkansas.

---------- I ----------

The One And Only

I WAS AN ONLY CHILD, BUT I WASN'T A LONELY CHILD.

I played sports, like basketball, with numerous friends and neighbors. It never entered my mind that I wanted or needed a brother and sister. You get used to being an only child, so you never think about it.

I always adapted to change, like when we moved to White Station in Memphis or when I went to summer camp every year or when I was sent away to prep school.

For instance, I went to Camp Carolina in Brevard, North Carolina, for two months every summer for six years until I was 14.

At first, I was a little bit homesick, but it was nothing I couldn't overcome. I loved the outdoors, and you could do everything in the outdoors and sporting world at Camp Carolina.

The big lakes, the clear water and the clean air were all things I enjoyed that I couldn't get in Memphis during the summer. Hiking (my least favorite activity), fishing and camping became part of my Camp Carolina life.

On special occasions and weekends, our counselors took us to Slippery Rock on the Davidson River. There, you could slide down this huge rock, 75 to 80 yards long and 30 yards wide. Cool spring water would run over the rock, and you'd drop into the swirling water below.

And it was cold, cold water.

The daily schedule gave me structure, and I've always liked structure. You got up at 6:30 in the morning, you made your bunk, you ate breakfast and then your bunk would be inspected.

About 9:30, you had hour-long activities like tennis, archery, rifle range, football, basketball, baseball and golf. At noon, you'd eat lunch, have a 90-minute rest period and then dive back into the activities until 6 o'clock when we'd eat dinner. We had a few activities after dinner and that was your day.

When camp was over for the summer, I looked forward to going home to Memphis. But when it was time to go back to Camp Carolina the next summer, I looked forward to going away again.

I've always been a very seasonal man. I've lived my life a season at a time. I can't wait for a season to come, but when it's over I move on.

I certainly had my share of fun in Memphis, especially since I started driving when I was 14. My childhood friend Jim Rainier, who was also my best man for my first marriage, remembers I had a lot of fun with my first set of wheels:

"Billy started driving supposedly just to go to school and to the grocery store. But he'd drive in people's yards just to see them scatter.

"He was total fun, made a joke out of anything. He would set up everything. If you wanted to go to Toddle House late at night for a cheeseburger and fries, he made sure it happened. If you wanted to go fishing, he was the leader. He'd get three or four of us, and go over to Arkansas and fish."

All my life, people thought I was a good multi-tasker. My boyhood friend Carlo Oates can attest to that:

"Billy's father Buck and my father Charles were cotton men on Front Street and great friends.

"So when I was 15 years old and didn't have a driver's license, Buck would say to my Dad, 'Why don't you let Carlo go duck hunting with Billy? Billy can drive.'

"So one of the times we were hunting we were running late. Billy had this Chevrolet and all the windows were rolled down.

"All of a sudden, he says, 'Oates, hold the wheel!' He dives into the back seat to get his shotgun. He hangs out of the window because there's a dove tracking alongside us.

"Boom! He shoots the dove. He says, 'Go get him.' I say, 'You want him, you go get him.' He said, 'No, roll the window up. Let's go.'"

The fact that I annually went away to Camp Carolina made it easy for me when my parents told me they were sending me away to a private school in Chattanooga called McCallie, a very strong Presbyterian prep school.

I didn't fuss, fight or argue. You just didn't do that with my parents. I knew it was coming and I wasn't going to win, so why argue?

They thought I'd get a better education at a private school and they were right. Yep, they were definitely right. I also got good discipline.

And I really wanted to go to McCallie, too.

I was spoiled as an only child, so the structure and discipline McCallie provided shaped me.

My three years at McCallie starting in the 10th grade gave me things that I have carried through life. McCallie taught me value, responsibility, appreciation of my parents, the importance of God in my life and great study habits.

Because of McCallie, I've had the ability to have total concentration of whatever endeavor I've undertaken.

My favorite subject was math. I know a lot of people don't like math, but I liked it. It carried over in the cotton business, because I was constantly trading on numbers.

I liked history, geography and foreign languages, but I didn't like physics and chemistry. I hated them.

I didn't take public speaking at McCallie until I was a senior, but I loved it. I wasn't really brave at first about standing in front of people and speaking. It was something I feared.

But once I got involved in it, it became sort of a second nature. It gave me the foundation for all the speeches I would go on in life to give.

I bet I've given more than 150 speeches, all different kinds, not just on cotton but on various subjects and before all types of audiences.

I write my speeches by hand before they get typed and I always practice my speeches in my bedroom in front of my dogs. If they don't fall asleep, I've written a winner.

My favorite teacher was William Presley, who eventually became one of McCallie's headmasters.

He was my English teacher. I respected him, not just because he was a great teacher, but he was also a fine Christian man who became one of my role models.

Also, J.P. McCallie, a religion teacher, was another role model. He eventually became one of the headmasters as well.

Arthur Lee "Major" Burns was another great McCallie teacher. He got his nickname because he ruled like a major. He was just called "Maj." The one thing you didn't want to see was a note in your mailbox that said, "Please see me. ALB." He had tremendous respect from all students. Wow, he was a really tough disciplinarian. But we loved him for it. His grandson Lee Burns is now McCallie's headmaster.

One of the things that made it easy to adapt to the structure at McCallie was we wore school military uniforms. I liked wearing the uniform.

I also made a friend for life at McCallie when I roomed my senior year with Frank Mitchener. Actually, we didn't first meet at McCallie, according to Frank:

"I first met Billy at Camp Carolina when we were about to become teenagers. It was strictly by luck that we were assigned as roommates at McCallie. Neither of us requested it. It just happened.

"Back in those days, he was just as competitive as he is now. He's maybe the most competitive human being I've ever known.

"I remember one time when I made an 'A' on a paper. I was so proud. I walked in our dormitory room, showed Billy the paper and said, 'Look here, I made an 'A.' He pulled out his paper and said, 'I beat you. I made an A plus.'

"There were a lot of ambitious boys at McCallie. I shared a study hall desk with Ted Turner, who went on to create his cable networks. Ted would spend his summers at his grandfather's house down here in my hometown of Sumner, Mississippi.

"There were a lot of Memphis boys at McCallie and a lot of them were very successful. But everything Billy did he did well. He was a really good overall athlete."

I made many other friends at McCallie, like Julian McCamy, who was a devoted teddy bear of a friend. He was from Dalton, Georgia, and settled into Atlanta where he was quite successful in the real estate business. We remained friends until the day he died.

I played football and basketball for McCallie. I was a starting guard in basketball, but I was a 140-pound fullback in football. I was slow as crap and I could take a beating, so they beat me up pretty good.

I can't say enough great things about McCallie. I always think of those days with a full heart. I wish I could say the same about my brief college stay at Vanderbilt, but can't.

I was a good tennis player, which came in handy when I went to Vanderbilt on a partial basketball scholarship.

After my first year at Vanderbilt, someone in the athletic department decided I was a much better tennis player than basketball player, so I was taken off the basketball scholarship and put on a tennis scholarship.

Vanderbilt turned out to be a disappointing experience. I wasn't a straight 'A' student, but I was pretty good. I had a teacher in accounting that gave me a 'D' and I thought I'd made an 'A.'

The reason I've never forgotten this is this was the first time that I had a life experience that I thought was unfair.

That teacher was a SOB who didn't like me. He was from Nashville, so students from Nashville did very well in his class. Someone like me from Memphis didn't do well. He was very prejudiced.

This event gave me a bad taste the rest of my life for Vanderbilt.

I lasted two years at Vanderbilt before I got married. My daddy said, 'Get your ass back to Memphis and go to work.'

The ironic thing is I left Vanderbilt just after talking Pete Nebhut, one of my Memphis friends who's also a cousin, into going to school there:

"Billy and I both had fathers in the cotton business. We became hunting and fishing buddies, even though I went to Central High in Memphis and he went to McCallie.

"Billy was always sort of hyper, a Type 'A' competitive guy who counted every fish he ever caught, every duck he ever killed.

"He was mischievous. He encouraged me to go to Vanderbilt, and he talked me into joining the SAE fraternity before I even got to school.

"Of course when I finally got to Vanderbilt, he was about to leave. He did give me a list of the girls in Nashville who were 'fast.' He gave me some good recommendations along those lines."

So for the next 1½ years, I went to class in the morning to finish my degree at the University of Memphis – it was Memphis State back then – and worked for my daddy in the afternoon.

It was good to get a college degree, but to me it was just paper. I had known from day one of my life that I wanted to be in the cotton business just like my daddy.

"I loved my daddy." — William Buchanan "Buck" Dunavant

2

The Buck Stops Here

FROM WHAT PEOPLE TELL ME, MY DADDY BUCK Dunavant was the best cotton man who ever lived.

In those days when you bought or sold cotton, you would look at a sample taken out of a 500-pound bale. My daddy was magnificent. He could walk in a cotton room on Front Street where they would have samples displayed on big tables. He'd pick up the cotton and look for two things. First, there was the grade, which involves the color and the leaf. Then, he'd examine the staple, which is the length of the fiber.

He was just very, very good at picking the right cotton, and as it turns out so was I. But I never could equal him in this area.

Daddy was a tough guy and didn't give you a lot of compliments. Your work proved to him what you could do and what you couldn't do.

Away from work, he was a quiet man who enjoyed the outdoors. Hunting and fishing were his passions, and he always wore a tie when doing either. Even outdoors, he was a well-dressed man.

My mother Dorothy had a tremendous personality. She was just playful and fun to be around. She was a dynamo. I first learned how to play tennis because she used to play at the University Club. She wasn't bad for a lady tennis player.

One of my grandmothers, my mother's mother, lived with us for several years. She was very prim and proper. One day when I was 16, I drove through the car wash with her, and right in the middle of the wash I let the windows down. I was just playing with her, but she got on my butt pretty good.

When I was 12 years old, my Daddy told me he would give me $25,000 if I didn't smoke or drink until I was 21. That was a lot of money in those days.

It was just part of my mindset not to do those things until I reached 21. I've never smoked in my life, but I've caught up on my drinking.

The maddest my Daddy ever got at me and the maddest I ever got at him was the time he thought I'd lied about something and I didn't and he beat the crap out of me.

Whenever he called me Billy, everything was fine. Whenever he called me "Son," I knew I had stepped in it somewhere.

From the time I was nine years old, I wanted to be in the cotton business. On weekends, I was exposed to other cotton men that Daddy did business with, and they were just full of it. They all enjoyed each other, whether it was hunting, fishing, drinking or working. They just enjoyed each other.

I liked what I saw and I wanted to be part of that group.

They had differences, but nothing ever serious. Their vocabulary was sprinkled with profanity, but the bond they formed in the cotton business was so trustworthy that it could never be broken.

Watching them with the love and respect they had for each other had such an impact on me.

When I was 19, I went to work for my Daddy and his partner T.J. White in their business T.J. White and Company. They had started the company in the early 1930s. Mr. White was 20 years older than my Dad, but they were equal partners and good friends, and Mr. White basically let my Dad run the company throughout its history.

Like most companies, it struggled through the depression years. The company specialized in premium styles of Memphis territory cotton and primarily shipped to the U.S textile industry. The company did little export business, yet still always made a profit on a very low volume of 40,000 to 60,000 bales

"Daddy Buck was a great skeet shot and always wore his hat, tie, and vest at the shooting competitions."

a year. There were about 12 employees to handle all the buying, classing, shipping, selling and billing.

I started out as a squidge, which is putting cotton samples in a tray after you decide on the grade and staple of the sample. My first salary was $50 per week and a year later it grew to $100 per week. Since I was married, my Dad supplemented my income with an extra $100 per week.

There was guy named Jim Nolan who was really my Daddy's protégé when I started working at T.J. White. Jim was more than 20 years older than me. He was with the company long before I came, and I was a little subconsciously jealous of that.

Being the competitor I was, I really wanted to outdo him. Once I started working, there was no holding back. That was just my nature. Jim and I, as can be expected, drifted apart. After about three years, he left the company.

I officially started with the company in 1952. By that time, the volume had grown to 75,000 bales per year. The company net profit climbed from $100,000 to $350,000 annually and was shared equally by partners.

In 1953, I was made a junior partner. I became a full-time partner in 1956, though I didn't share in the profits.

Daddy always designated me as the guy who entertained clients. I didn't drink or smoke back then, but clients had to be entertained. My butt would take them to dinner, stay with them and do everything they wanted to do.

One of those guys was Arthur Sharp, a Harvard graduate who bought cotton for a textile company called Bemis Brothers Bag Company. He lived in Taunton, Massachusetts. His wife was East Coast prim-and-proper, and I'm sure he was a perfect man up there.

But when he came to Memphis, he'd get drunk as four owls every day and every night. He was probably 20 years older than my father, but he loved my Daddy.

Daddy didn't mess with him. When he came to town, it was, "Son, take care of Mr. Sharp." So I took care of Mr. Sharp.

Though he was in his early 60s and about 40 years older than me, we became fast friends because we both liked to hunt and fish. Mr. Sharp loved both, but primarily hunting. He gave me a collection of guns and then I bought another collection from him years later.

He never talked bad, but he had his vices in Memphis. He'd get drunk at Hatchie Coon, a duck hunting club about 90 minutes outside Memphis where we'd go sometimes to spend the night. Those were the days before I drank, so I had to sit there and watch him get drunk.

One morning at 5 o'clock, I went to pick him up at The Peabody because we were going duck hunting. He'd normally meet me at the side entrance. But on this day, he wasn't there.

All the bellmen at the hotel knew Mr. Sharp well. I asked the bellmen standing at the door, "Have y'all seen Mr. Sharp?" They said, "No, he hasn't come down yet."

So I go with a bellman to Mr. Sharp's room so he can let me in. We get inside and his bed is empty. We go into the bathroom, and there he is in the tub.

He's sound asleep and the water is up to his chin. Every time he snores, water ripples all the way down the tub.

I finally got him out of the tub, dressed him and took him duck hunting. He was fine after that. But he was some kind of a hell-raiser.

Somebody else who worked for Bemis was a buyer in Jackson, Tennessee, named Waring Hazelhurst, who many years later joined Dunavant Enterprises. We hit it off from the very beginning.

Maybe it was because we shared a love of cotton and hunting, which Waring remembers came together one day when I was delivering some cotton to a Bemis mill in Jackson:

"This mill had a lot of pigeons that were a nuisance. So when Billy was delivering some cotton to the mill and he saw all those pigeons, he talked to the mills about shooting them. We arranged to have a pigeon shoot with four or five people, but the main shooter was Billy.

"He must have killed almost 100 pigeons. We put them all in a tote sack and were trying to figure out how to get rid of them.

"Billy came up to our house for supper that night. We said, 'Billy, take this tote sack with you, and somewhere between here and Memphis throw it out.'

"Well, apparently, he couldn't throw the pigeons out of his car fast enough. The next morning, there was a line of dead pigeons leading out of town."

"My daddy loved fishing more than hunting. He's pictured here with a nice catch at Veradero Beach, Cuba, on May 30, 1956."

I'll never forget the first time in 1954 my Daddy sent me to Front Street to buy cotton. He described the kind of cotton we needed and told me to go down to the Berry Brooks Cotton Company. He wanted me to look at a 650-bale lot that had been described to him. It sounded like it was what we wanted.

So I went down there, classed the cotton and made a bid. As it turned out, I bought a whole lot of cotton.

The next morning, the samples of my purchase were rolled out in our cotton room. My Dad asked to see the samples of my purchase. We were looking at it when Mr. White walked in the room.

My purchase was not exactly what I thought I bought. It was leafy and spotted.

Mr. White looked at my purchase, asked what I paid and my dad told him. Mr. White replied, "Buck, we could have sent the boy through Harvard for what this cotton is going to cost this company."

To this day, I think since I was a novice as a cotton buyer, the Berry Brooks sellers switched the samples on me. My buying improved greatly after that first experience.

Daddy taught me many things. One of his first lessons was every day in the cotton business is a new day. If you screw up, put it behind you and start the next day.

All my life, I've used Daddy's philosophy to move on to the next day after a bad day. When things go wrong, you shake the dust from your feet, you learn from it and you go forward. I took that advice to heart, because I screwed up many times.

Like the time I wanted to learn how to farm to better understand my customers. I bought 4,500 acres in Tallahatchie County, Mississippi. I found out pretty quick I was a terrible farmer, so I sold half of the property.

I also learned that the cotton business was definitely a business built on trust. My Dad was known to be a trustworthy man in making deals. Deals were done with handshakes and contracts were eventually written. When we did write them, we rarely changed anything we had agreed upon with a handshake.

Trust was just a way of life, a way of doing business.

There was never a doubt who was going to eventually take over the company. Mr. White retired in 1960, eight years after I went to work there.

For several years, I had encouraged Dad to increase our volume and our profits grew. I was very aggressive as I learned the business.

Dad and I agreed that if we were to grow substantially, we had to increase our volume and expand our business outside the U.S. Mr. White also wanted to grow the company, yet he quickly realized the risk factor had increased. So he retired, but he left his money on deposit with the company just in case we went belly up so his money could pay off our debts.

I always wondered why he retired. The deposit he left us showed he had confidence that Dad and I wouldn't financially hurt him.

With Mr. White out of the picture, we renamed the company W.B. Dunavant and Company.

Banks had great confidence in my Dad's ability, so financing was not a problem. We dealt with the First National Bank of Memphis, and we had adequate lines of credit to grow our company.

By 1959, the year before Mr. White retired, I was beginning to run the company because my Dad's health was not excellent. Then in January 1961, he had a stroke and passed away.

Suddenly, at age 29, I was left to own and run the company.

Being a cotton merchant entailed quite a big risk. You had to borrow money from the banks to buy the cotton. Then you would sell the cotton and try to deliver the cotton to the cotton mills overseas and to North and South Carolina where most of the mills were located.

My Daddy died at that time of the year in November, December and January when we were usually in debt from borrowing money from the bank to finance the cotton we were buying.

The bank was very nervous that year because my Dad, probably the best cotton man that had ever been in history, was gone. We had just purchased a sizeable amount of cotton out of the CCC loan stocks and we did not have the cotton sold. We were long about 75,000 bales and the futures market was not a viable hedge at the time.

We were a little company, and we owed the bank $25 million to $30 million. The bank didn't know if I could carry it out or not. I never doubted I could, but there were some anxious moments.

I went down to visit the bank and explain my game plan. The bank was beginning to build confidence in my ability to merchandise and agreed to keep financing our company. We sold the cotton over a 60-day period and did well on the purchase.

From that point, we were off and running.

I kept the banks posted on everything I was doing, and they watched my every move. They always knew the direction I was headed.

It was a direction that eventually took us far beyond the limits of our imaginations. But the success would have not been possible without the combination of my Dad and Mom.

Dad taught me to be firm, that trust started with a handshake and the value of honesty meant more than anything else in a business that is built on relationships.

Mom balanced that by teaching me to be sentimental, to never meet a stranger and to be a fun-loving person who jokes.

Each added a dimension to shape me into the cotton man I became.

Billy classing cotton in Memphis with his Chinese customers.

---------- 3 ----------

Fine China

MY FATHER WAS A DOMESTIC COTTON MERchant. We just bought and sold cotton in the United States, but there were only so many markets in our country.

Until about 1965, our U.S. profit margins were very small because we had no free market. All cotton basically was traded to loan level.

When I took over the company, I went from thinking just about the short term to projecting long-range goals. I knew if we were to grow we had to be an international company. A lot of our big competitors were international. We had to go to the world market.

I was inspired to have this vision by an older friend named Ned Cook, who originally had a cotton company called Cook and Company. Ned had an immense vision that he wanted to have the biggest company in the world, but he couldn't compete with us.

So he got out of the cotton business and into the grain business. As Cook Industries, he developed into an excellent soybean trader. Ned had that vision to make more and do more, and he did. He was a man with big thoughts, big ideas, and I always respected him for that.

His vision made me look at the big picture that extended far beyond the U.S. borders.

With the world market, you had southern and northern hemisphere crops that you harvested at different times of the year. It wasn't steady all year. The summer months of July and

August were slow months because foreign cotton wasn't moving in volumes at that time either.

President Richard Nixon and Secretary of State Henry Kissinger renewed diplomatic relations with China in 1972, and our company was the first to break back into China when we sold them 150,000 bales. It had been 25 or 30 years since the U.S. had done any cotton business with China.

Through a French company called Louie Dreyfus Commodities located in Paris, they introduced us into China by doing joint ventures. Having a go-between was beneficial in the early days. But once we began to know the people, we did our own thing.

We had lots of good experiences with the Chinese, but they were tough negotiators. They tried to tire you and break you down. The first couple of years I went over there in 1973 and 1974, you'd go over planning on spending two days trading with them and you'd be there eight, nine, 10 days.

You'd have a meeting for 30 to 45 minutes every day. They wanted me to be there at an appointed time and you weren't there long. You had to get right to the point.

The meeting would break up and you'd be left sitting there in the Beijing Hotel, not knowing anybody since I rarely took employees with me. I often made the trip alone because it was easy to negotiate and I knew what I wanted to do.

The Chinese did like to keep an eye on you. Jim Gilliland, my longtime personal attorney, recalls the time I decided to go jogging in Beijing:

"Billy has this nervous energy. If he doesn't exercise, he gets to be a bear.

"So he gets off the plane in Beijing, his internal clock is upside down. He wants to get exercise when he gets to his hotel. He pulls on his shorts, puts on his running shoes and off he goes running through the streets of Beijing.

Signing the Chinese cotton sales agreement at Billy's office in Memphis.

"After awhile, he looks behind him and sees a Chinese guy in a suit and street shoes running like hell.

"The next day, Billy received a note from someone in authority that said, 'Please Mr. Dunavant don't go running in the streets of Beijing without asking us first.'

"I can imagine the poor Chinese guy there who was assigned to look after Billy running three or four miles in his street shoes."

There was a trip to China in 1979 that we took a group with us. Sam Reeves, my Dunavant Enterprises co-partner and manager of my California operation, remembers we took a group for a good reason:

"The reason that the Chinese wanted to deal with Americans is history teaches us revolutions result in major shortages of food and fiber. China was looking to the outside world for both and the

best place to come for food and fiber was the United States. China needed massive amounts of product.

"So in the spring of 1979 by the time the U.S and China had formed a formal diplomatic relationship and we were able to deal more directly with China, Billy was invited to come to China by Chinatex, a cotton buying organization.

"Part of this was brokered by David Hardoon, Billy's agent in Hong Kong. The Hardoon name was one of the prominent names in China for the past several hundred years. He brokered this because he's very close to the Chinese, partially because of his relationship, but partially because Billy was the largest merchant in the world. So we knew it was special for them.

"If both Billy and I had gone to China together, and nothing happened with a deal, that would have sent a red flag to competitors to be careful of the market.

"So the way we did it for appearance purposes was we made it appear it was a tourist trip. Billy took his second wife Ann and several children, I took my wife Betsy and several of my children. Johnny Dobbs took his wife and several children.

"At that time, many Chinese had never seen Westerners. So when we went out on the streets, we were an attraction. Polaroid cameras had just come out, so we'd take pictures of the Chinese and give them the pictures. Many of them had never seen themselves in a photo, so it almost became where we couldn't do it anymore because we caused a disruption. Every time we went out on the street, we had 50 to 100 people surrounding us.

"We were probably the only U.S cotton merchant that had been invited directly, so we had daily meetings with Mr. Mao of Chinatex and his people negotiating the sale. We realized that there was going to be the potential of a large purchase and we had prepared ourselves in advance to bring along a bunch of cotton in anticipation that something was going to be taking place.

"We finished the sale on a Friday, and it was a huge sale. In fact it was more than 3 percent of all the cotton grown in the

United States. To put that into perspective, any time you get a 3 or 4 percent change in a commodity, it can cause huge market volatility dislocation. We had been prepared for this.

"We finish the negotiation. We're all ecstatic.

"And then Mr. Mao says, 'Would you like to double the order?'

"All of a sudden, we've gone from something that could dislocate the market, to something that could cause a massive dislocation with a 6 to 7 to 8 percent change.

"To Billy's credit, without flinching or showing his hand, he said, 'Look, let's think about this. Can you give us an option on the second order, we'll confirm the first? We'll give an option of about a week, let us go with everything.' They agreed to that.

"In those days, many people hadn't dealt with China. There was no arbitration. You didn't know what this was quite about. Would they just give this order, try to double it and go to competitors to do the same thing, which would have caused a massive movement in the market?

"We've got to get back to the United States to execute this deal. Billy had to stay because he was the No. 1 in the country. My family stayed, but I feigned illness and immediately caught the first plane.

"I had no luggage, no nothing. Just a dop kit. Got the first flight out of Beijing to Tokyo, Tokyo to Hawaii and Hawaii to San Francisco, California arriving at 7:10 in the morning. The market in New York was opening at 7:30. At that point, you start buying the futures and then buy all the spots we could.

"By end of the next week, Billy was still in China. He confirmed the second part of the sale. When the word got out, the market was stunned about a sale of that size (almost 200,000 bales). A sale of that size has never happened, particularly with China. That may be the most amazing event that became a part of the Dunavant lore."

It was a long and tough negotiation. My personal attorney Jim Gilliland recalls it got nit-picky at the end, because we were trying to complete the deal and keep it quiet:

"Billy and I didn't know anything what was ahead. There was no contract we could look at to give us a checklist or what we needed to cover as we put the deal together. He said, 'Put together what you can, let's talk about this thing real real close.'

"We realized leaking the news to anybody was an invitation to bankrupt Dunavant. Billy had his best friend Eli Tullis buy a huge amount of cotton to begin covering the Chinese order, but Billy couldn't tell him what it was for. Eli called Billy and said, 'You've got to tell me why I'm buying this cotton. I'm exposing myself. My banks don't like it. You've got to tell me. We're friends.'

"What Eli didn't know was that I was on the other side telling Billy, 'I'll wring your damned neck if you whisper anything to anybody about this sale.'

"The deal finally got down to one point. We insisted on international inspection of cotton at the port. When you put a bale of cotton on the ship and you sail that mother all the way across the Pacific Ocean, then the cotton weighs different from what it weighed in San Francisco.

"That's called franchising the cotton. Somebody who inspects the cotton may find different characteristics from the temperature, the moisture. We knew all those things.

"China counters saying, 'We won't have any international inspectors in China, so that's a deal-breaker.' We say, 'We have to inspect the cotton because we're not going to expose ourselves to some bureaucrat at Chinatex telling us what he thinks the component of the cotton is at the time it's received.'

"They come back with a compromise saying, 'Mr. Dunavant can come to Beijing anytime and inspect any cotton he ships over there.'

Billy would jog every morning through the streets of Beijing during the Chinese negotiations.

"Billy wasn't going to China to inspect the friggin' bales. At that point, we decided to take the risk and do the deal without demanding the inspection.

"In the end through Billy's talent and preparation, forward contracting made the deal. The reason is you can't hedge your position enough on the exchange to do the deal. If you sold futures, it would disrupt.

"How do you buy $100 million or more in cotton as an agent on the exchange? You can't do it. So Billy exposed himself to an uncovered liability to acquire all this cotton. If the cotton price moved on him, he was dead.

"The deal changed the cotton industry, it changed regulations. It changed Billy from just another small street broker into a dominant player in the cotton industry. He did it all by himself. Billy's energy, personality and the relationships he had unique to him made it possible.

"Billy had made the largest hit in cotton market history. Cotton went from 30 cents a pound to $1 a pound. When market was going up, we were called to go to New York City to appear before the Commodities Futures Trading Commission, an independent government agency that regulates futures and options markets.

"They were saying Billy was long, he was squeezing everybody in the industry and it look like the deal might be illegal.

"A lot of that was based on perception. Nobody knew Billy Dunavant. His company had been a little guy on Front Street until all this came along.

"We knew there were anti-cornering positions in the law, so we were damned sure we had a justifiable marketing position. We had to defend everything. Billy explained it all, and they bought it.

"The sale moved the earth. It tripled the price of cotton and people out there were left short because they had to keep meeting their margins. It was very de-stablizing.

"The market had gotten so high that some people were filing bankruptcy. So Billy eased off and we left millions on the table. It was a right thing to do."

The sales just got bigger. A major reason we were successful in China was David Hardoon, who operated our Far East operations in Hong Kong.

Whether it was dealing with Chinatex and later the Chinese national reserve, David was instrumental in our company closing three deals for 1 million or more bales. He worked for me from 1986 until 2010 when I sold my cotton business, and he feels strongly we made history that will be hard to top:

"I don't think what Dunavant Enterprises did will ever be duplicated, because the structure of the Chinese cotton business has changed.

"Back then in the late 1980s, the 1990s and early in the 2000s, Chinatex or the Chinese national reserve were the only companies buying. Dunavant Enterprises accounted for 95 to 100 percent of the sales, so we actually took care of China's entire requirement.

"Dunavant had a reputation of being a very reliable company. China wanted to find a company it could entrust with most or all of its sales. Can this company deliver on time? Can it provide the right quality of cotton?

"I'd built a relationship through the years with Mao Binglin, who was a middle-level executive at Chinatex. My job was to convince him we would deliver, that if we were committed to you that our word was our bond.

"In our deal together in 1990, there was an overnight bid from Chinatex every single night for four months. A bid was never less than 20,000 bales, but sometimes it went to 50,000 and 75,000.

"Putting all these deals together was quite challenging. Billy gave me his telephone number and said, 'I don't care what time it is. You call me whenever something is happening.'

"The difficult part was to tell Chinatex that we knew they wanted to buy a huge amount of cotton. But if they spread the business to two or three companies, the chance that they'd be able to buy that huge quantity would be lessened. It's because everybody on the selling side would be competing against each other to acquire the cotton on the interior and perhaps hedge their positions in futures.

"We had to convince Chinatex we were big enough to handle their requirements, so they needed to give us a certain period of time to complete the deal exclusively.

"So I got the bids every night, and Billy would buy cotton. Some days, he would buy quite a bit of cotton. Other days, he'd be out of the market.

"It took a long time to find out how much cotton Chinatex wanted to buy. I remember one time after a long night of drink-

Billy and Chinese negotiator Mao Binglin signing
the major U.S./China sales agreement.

ing, Mao Binglin held up two hands. I said, 'Two hands meaning 1 million bales?' He didn't say anything but 'Two hands.'

"I called Billy right away and told him. He asked, 'What does two hands mean?' I said, 'One million bales.'

"We satisfied their entire requirements that year.

"It took us four months to acquire the first half million bales and about three to four months for the second half million bales. The hard part was this whole exercise required confidentiality.

"There was a lot of camouflaging going on. Our competitors were digging around for information. The rumor was going around that Dunavant was buying cotton in the interior and paying these kinds of prices.

"But we had a pact. We weren't going to say anything and Chinatex wasn't, though Mao got a lot of heat from people calling him to see if something was going on.

"Later on Easter Friday 2004, I got a call from Madam Lehe, who was in charge of the Chinese national reserve. I'd gotten to know her through the years.

"I ended up meeting her in Beijing in my hotel suite. She was interested in stocking up the national reserve. Same thing as our Chinatex deal. We needed time to buy what they needed and confidentiality. It took us half a year, and I also had to convince Madam Lehe that we would have to buy cotton from around the world, not just the U.S., to get the grade of cotton they wanted.

"This sale was around 1.6 million bales, and it really pissed off our competition because they had no sniff at this business."

Part of doing business with the Chinese was drinking with them when you completed a deal. They fill your glass up, there would be the toast 'KANPAI!' Then they'd fill your glass up again. You try not to do too much of it or it will make you triple drunk.

One night, we're drinking stuff that tasted like lighter fluid. The Chinese would do a toast, and I just kept pouring the drink on the floor. They'd immediately fill it back up, because they think you're trying to get out of it.

When I stood to get up, my feet were stuck where I'd poured my drinks. The stuff had taken the varnish off the wooden floor.

Once the Chinese got on board, their word became their bond also. We got to be good friends. We had them down to Mississippi to Quail Hollow. They duck hunted, they fished. We did everything with them.

Hunting with the Chinese was a risky proposition. They didn't know how to shoot a gun any more than would a monkey. You'd give them a lecture about safety, and they'd fire a shotgun right by your head. We nearly got our heads blown off two or three times.

One night in Washington in the 1990s, they got Tommie fall-down drunk and she ended up breaking her jaw and mouth. It wasn't funny at the time, but it did get the deal done as Tommie recalls:

"The Chinese have a thing they do where they pick on somebody at a dinner party and make that person drink. On this night, they picked on me. I was sitting next to David Hardoon. I kept saying, 'I don't want to do this.' He and Billy kept saying, 'You have to, you have to, the deal depends on it.'

"I got plowed and fell on my face, breaking my jaw. Billy sold the cotton, and I didn't get any workman's compensation, but that was part of dealing with the Chinese. They loved him, they respected his company being a family company. They believed Billy at his word. They always wanted to deal with him."

The Chinese were unusual how they did business. If they wanted to buy a million bales from you, they'd start out at 200 or 400. Then as you get involved in trading with them, they'd gradually increase the volume.

In October 1990, we sold 1,000,000 bales in one sale to the Chinese. It's the biggest deal anyone had ever made in the world at the time. I closed that deal on the way to board the plane to come home to Memphis. We had been negotiating for a week and couldn't make any progress, so I left.

They weren't going to let me leave. They knew they were going to make a deal, but I didn't. I'm walking and talking and they finally said, "We got a deal." And I said, "Okay." They said, "You want to double it?" I said, "Yeah." They didn't want to triple it, but we doubled it. It was a great trip.

This sale to China put us on the map, and I mean worldwide. It made our future for we went from being a cotton merchant to THE cotton merchant.

With China, sometimes we made a lot of money and sometimes we just did the business for fun, just to keep your name in front of them. We only had one bad year with them when they didn't keep their word and it cost us $15 million. By the time I retired in 2005, we were selling China more than 1.3 million bales per year.

After we started in China, every move we made in the international market spread out a little more than previously. Most of our international deals were tenuous, but most all of them worked out. A lot had to do with the personal relationships we developed with these people within these companies and countries.

South Korea was the easiest country for negotiations. We were one of the first to grow the Korean market. We were No. 1 in Korea for 25 years. They were very honorable people.

In choosing countries in which to expand, we studied where consumption was growing. It was obvious that China's population was going to grow faster than anybody else. So we first zeroed in on China.

Maybe we took a few risks internationally that we shouldn't have taken. But one that worked for almost 10 years was when I bought the Zambian cotton operations of Lonrho in 1999.

We weren't real strong in Africa at that time. That was an opportunity to get in the fixed asset business. We bought a gin, farms, the warehouses, the whole bit. We were in total control. Russ Cherry, our Dunavant Enterprises attorney, recalls our Zambia operation as a real adventure:

"When we bought the operation from Lonrho, we started financing individual farmers who didn't have $50 to their names. We would put together a 10-quart bucket with seed, fertilizer, chemicals for insecticide, a sprayer and tools.

"Then we would teach them how to grow cotton. We hired 286 trainers and they each supervised 10 lead farmers who then each

would work with 15 neighbors. It took two to three months to get a farmer fully trained on how to be productive.

"We had trucks go around all over the country to deliver these buckets, to help with the farmers, to train them how to grow cotton. We had a collection system. We not only had the trucks to pick up the cotton, we had it weighed and an armed guard would pay the farmer right on the spot. You're talking a lot of money traveling all over Africa to Zambia to out in the bush.

"It might take two or three weeks to cover the country because you're stopping at your mail routes so to speak and dealing with the farmers, who liked it because they were paid in cash. They were getting $150 to $200 a year extra that they didn't have to buy food with, since most of what they raised were beans and corn to eat. This was money for them that they were able to increase their standard of living.

"We realized we were landlocked in Zambia, had a lot of cotton and there was a cost to get the cotton to port in Durban to export it to the Far East and India where they were making fabric. So we partnered up with some South Africans and bought a trucking company to truck cotton from Zambia.

"The truck company had trucks going into Zambia with general commodities such as toothpaste, toilet paper, almost anything you could consume. Since those trucks would be empty after unloading, we worked out a system that they'd come out with our cotton and take it to the port.

"We had good managers. They started realizing these trucks, like two 18-wheelers attached together, would disappear for a day or two. What was happening is these truckers would go on side roads at different villages and have sex with prostitutes. Our truck full of cotton is sitting there and we were losing time.

"So we put GPS on trucks so we knew where they were. The truckers knew they couldn't get off the main highway, so we had a more efficient operation.

"Something else we did was finance sexual education programs and medical programs to fight AIDs. We started that after noticing the farmers that we had dealt with one year weren't there the next year. They were dying of AIDS.

"Zambia worked out well until we sold the company. We were the largest employer of people in Zambia for a number of years.

"One of the secrets of Billy's international success was that he usually hired local people in the locale he had a business operation. He always thought it was better to manage it that way, because managers with local ties always knew customs, people and language. They were able to cut through barriers quicker than if Billy hired Americans.

"Billy hired managers that had a lot of respect, who were good at what they did working for other companies. But they wanted to come work for him because they had more of a free rein. They liked they weren't being micromanaged."

I never was a big believer in doing something I didn't know anything about. I did some of that and most of that was not successful. If I knew something about it, I was normally very successful. But if I didn't, a lot of it fell on its ass.

A few years after I bought the cotton operations in Lonhro, I bought a small Ugandan company. I did the same thing I did in Zambia. I kept the company's native management team, because it kept things relatively smooth with local leaders.

We stuck with what we knew internationally. And the managers I put around me were molded the same way, doing things they knew something about.

I had good help around the world, and they dealt with problems you can't imagine. Rickard Laurin, who managed our office in Geneva, acquired properties for us overseas. He recalls the time he built two gins for our company in the country of Tajikistan:

President Ronald Reagan greets Billy at the White House during Billy's China negotiations.

"We built the gins, but when we started to operate them a warlord came down and told our gins manager, 'Listen, my friend, every 10th wagon out of here is mine.' This manager was in shock. So I flew in to talk to the warlord face-to-face.

"This warlord said, 'This is the way it is.' I said, 'I can't do that, this is against U.S. regulations.' He said, 'We don't have any rules in this country. I need to survive and I need to take care of shit, so I need 10 percent of what's coming out of your factory.' I said, 'Sorry, can't do that. You can buy the two gins for 50 cents on the dollar. I can't run this operation with this situation going on.'

"After a long negotiation, we got the price down to 50 percent of the value and I sold him the gins."

The major challenge as we were growing, especially internationally, was doing business with people who would honor contracts. That has been a major burden in my years in the cotton industry, as well as everybody else's. When price fluctuations are very violent, up or down, there are many defaults. If you've got something sold to somebody, they just say, "The price went the wrong way, I ain't gonna pay you."

We've been very blessed that we had a minimal amount of those kinds of failures. We always got to be good friends with the people we did business with all over the world.

Billy fiercely contested matches against Canadian Davis Cup tennis star John Bassett. Bassett owned the Memphis Southmen football team in the 1970s.

4

In It To Win It

I'VE ALWAYS LOVED TO COMPETE, WHETHER IT WAS IN business, on the tennis court and golf course, or in a duck blind, deer stand or mountain stream.

I've mellowed a lot, but I'm still very, very competitive, even about trivial things. I just have to win but I won't ever cheat to win.

When I go hunting, I will kill more birds than anybody else. I will catch more fish than anybody else and I will be damned unhappy if I don't. It's no secret I'm a poor loser. Everyone knows this about me, especially wife Tommie:

"If you're walking with Billy, he's got to be the one walking the fastest. He's got to catch the most fish. If we are turkey hunting with other people, he's got to kill more turkeys. If he misses a shot and starts cussing, you don't know if he's talking to the gun or himself, so you just start backing up. He's thrown plenty of guns in anger in one of the lakes in Quail Hollow. He pouts when he loses."

My friends, like Chuck Smith, also know:

"Myself and a partner who was a complete unknown were playing in a club tennis tournament. In the first round, we had to play Billy, who won the tournament almost every year forever. His partner was a good player, but somehow we beat them.

"The next morning, the phone rings and the voice on the other end says, 'Hey Chuck, this is Billy.' I'm thinking Billy's never called me this early in the morning.' So I said, 'C'mon, who is

this really?' The voice said, 'This is Billy, you want to play tennis today?' I said, 'Sure.' He said, 'We're gonna play at noon at The Racquet Club. I'll see you out there.'

"So I go there, we play two sets and he whips me like a stepchild. It's embarrassing. It's like 6-0, 6-1. I don't want to do anything but get out of there as quick I can.

"I come to the net, shake Billy's hand and say, 'Thank you so much. I really enjoyed that.' He said, 'We're not through.' I said, 'You just beat me in two straight sets. It's kinda over.' He said, 'No, we're gonna play another set.' So we play a third set, and he beats me 6-0."

I didn't lose too often, but my friend Neely Mallory remembers a time where he found a way to beat me at golf:

"Four couples went on a tennis trip to Puerto Rico. We played tennis for three days and of course Billy wins all three days.

"He says, 'Neely, tomorrow we're going to play golf.' He had about a five-handicap. He said, 'I'm going to take the two non-tennis players and we're going to play a scramble. You're gonna play us.'

I said, 'One stipulation. I get to throw the ball one time per hole.' Billy agrees.

On the first hole, they putt six inches from the hole. I said, 'Mark it.' I putted up to about a foot to the hole and they gave me the putt. I said, 'Now, I'm going to take my throw.' I said, 'Give me one of your golf balls.'

"They did, and I turned from where their putt was marked and threw their ball in the lake. They made a double bogey 6 on the hole and we made a par 4.

"It was bedlam the next few holes. They were throwing clods of dirt at me.

"Every once in awhile, it's fun to beat Billy."

Steve Ehrhart, the former president/general manager of my USFL team the Memphis Showboats and now executive director of the AutoZone Liberty Bowl, remembers the time I called the bluff of NBA legend Jerry West, who spent a few seasons in Memphis as president of the Grizzlies:

"Billy had consummate confidence as a competitor. There was the day I brought Jerry West over to meet Billy at one of those office business lunches. The Grizzlies had just hired Jerry.

"The conversation got around to golf. Jerry West is a very confident person. Billy asked Jerry, 'What's your handicap?' Jerry said, 'I'm a zero, I don't have a handicap, maybe plus one.'

"Billy's competitive juices kick in. He tells Jerry, 'Maybe we can play, maybe put on a little wager.' As soon as Billy says that, Jerry immediately backs off, saying, 'I'll need some time to warm up.'

"Here's Billy meeting one of the world's great athletes for the first time and he challenges him to play golf for money. Jerry West never did play Billy."

I grew up as a kid playing golf and tennis. I started playing tennis, because my mother played. I was pretty damned good and I probably could have made something out of myself as a tennis player if I hadn't played golf as much as I played tennis.

I was better at golf than any sport I played. I never was offered a golf scholarship anywhere. I couldn't hit it out of my shadow, but I could hit it straight every time. A good drive for me was 225 yards. I could chip like a maniac, but I couldn't putt worth a crap.

Late in the afternoon in our big side yard at our house, I used to go out and hit golf balls. My daddy would come out to watch and talk a bunch of shit, so one day I threw it back at him.

I said, "Let's see you hit some."

He puts the ball on the tee, swings, the ball sails across the street and breaks the window of our neighbor's house. My daddy is so embarrassed that he makes me go over and apologize for breaking the window like it was my fault.

I got down to a 4-handicap, maybe a 3, but one day in my 30s I quit golf. It just took too much time to play. Since I had played tennis in college for Vanderbilt and Memphis and played on the junior Davis Cup team, I started getting serious about tennis again.

Most people start out playing tennis and switch to golf as they get older. I did it the other way around and I went all in on tennis.

I tried to get the Memphis Country Club to buy that church next to them on Southern Avenue so tennis courts could be built. I told them I would finance it. It was really a good deal, but they just would never buy into it. So as always, I immediately moved on to the next thing.

I bought the old Memphis Athletic Club, tore it down and rebuilt it as The Racquet Club. I wanted to give Memphis a pro tennis tournament. I borrowed an idea from football, built skyboxes and we attracted the national indoor championships.

Now I didn't make a lot of money out of that, but I made money in other ways because the club catapulted us into other areas of development like condominium residential properties.

I was very proud of The Racquet Club. I wanted to offer a place for people to join, especially if they weren't approved for a country club membership.

The Racquet Club added something to Memphis, which usually was what always motivated me to get involved in something other investors might pass on. I was fortunate to hire Mac Winker to run it for me. As is the case with many people I hired, he became more than an employee. He became a lifelong friend, and Mac says he feels the same way:

"In the latter part of 1977, I was contacted by the search firm of Spencer Stewart and Associates out of Chicago, Illinois, to con-

sider a job in Memphis. As it turns out, Billy Dunavant had a private club called The Racquet Club of Memphis that had fallen far below his expectations.

"He made several attempts to fix this problem and was at the point where he was going to allow 'one more shot' to someone. If that person failed, he was either going to sell the club or turn it over to The Club Corporation of America, a firm that took over distressed private club properties.

"As Billy put it so beautifully, once he saw that I had all the credentials necessary to become Chairman of the Board at The Racquet Club, he asked Tommy Buford, the tennis director at that time, if he would find out if I could play tennis.

"Tommy quickly reported that I 'couldn't play a lick', so Billy immediately hired me.

"For me, Mac Winker, it turned out to be the opportunity of a lifetime. At the same time, for Billy Dunavant, for Dunavant Enterprises, for The Racquet Club and its employees, for Memphis, for St. Jude Children's Research Hospital and for the Mid-South region, it turned out to be an excellent decision as well.

The club quickly grew and became the place to be, the place to be seen, and a place where one should belong for exercise, business and pleasure. The Racquet Club was a feather-in-the-cap for all involved and I knew Billy Dunavant was proud of its development.

"It was during this time I discovered that Billy's word was golden. Once I told him I was working on getting a sponsorship from a certain bank. He told me that there was no possible way that particular bank would become a sponsor and went on to say 'If you do get one from them, I'll buy you a hat!'

"Well, I got the bank to sponsor and the next day I had a delivery from Billy at the front desk of The Racquet Club. To my surprise, enclosed was a very distinguished looking felt hat.

"I could see Billy laughing at his own gesture! The reality was that he was just keeping his word. What a lesson in life!

"Billy was great in communicating his wishes and then letting go as long as it reflected well on his company, the city and was good for the employees.

"So many firsts happened with The Racquet Club. The first executive suites (in the world) exclusively to watch tennis, the first major laundry (it served other clubs, churches, caterers, etc.) in a private club, and the first club in Memphis to construct tennis courts from scratch for private owners.

"Billy was tough and had a special eye for talent. He was a wonderful mentor and so gracious along the way.

"He sold me the club and the tournament after 14 years of working for him and even gave me a private loan to complete the package. He believed in me. I selected St. Jude to be our official charity and the club prospered. Billy and his company always supported the club. He was always interested in the club's progress and what was new on the table.

"We continued to grow our friendship and I added the woman's tournament which was another prize for the region. It seemed that each year there was a new internationally known champion.

"Every now and then I would even beat him at tennis. On my 60th birthday, he told the large gathering that he hired me because he knew he could easily beat me at tennis and now he was 'retiring' his tennis racquet as I was starting to beat him.

"That same night he said, 'Mac came to Memphis as an employee of Dunavant Enterprises, but now was a close personal friend.'

"Looking back at what The Racquet Club meant to me, my family and to the club's employees, for the city, the region and St. Jude, to be called Billy's friend was one of my best accomplishments of all.

"I loved him then and I love him now. After all, he's my friend!"

Billy congratulates Tracy Austin as she receives her championship trophy at The Racquet Club in Memphis.

The Racquet Club also gave me a daily respite from my hectic deal-filled mornings. When I wasn't out-of-town, I'd leave my office at 11:30, play a singles match daily starting at noon and be back at my office between 1:45 to 2:15.

I wanted to convince pro tennis to make The Racquet Club the host of the annual U.S. National Indoor championship tour stop. I knew the prestige of tennis in Memphis would improve greatly.

So I found the best man for the job, Donald Dell, former Davis Cup captain and founder of ProServ, one of the first sports marketing firms in the U.S. Quickly, Donald helped obtain the majority of the tournament's sponsorship dollars from outside of Memphis.

We were able to increase prize money, contribute to the players' pension fund and provide all the perks needed to attract the best players in the world. Donald recalls we made a pretty good team from the start when he was able to get the National Indoor Tournament to move to Memphis in 1977:

"I first met Billy when he owned The Racquet Club and it was hosting a pro tour tournament in the 1970s which was called in those days the U.S.T.A. National Indoor Championships. I was doing marketing, handling the TV rights for the club and probably for about 20 years did the TV commentating for the tournament.

"Billy and I just hit it off. Our personalities jelled.

"He had a fabulous reputation for integrity and honesty. He's one of the most honorable persons I know.

"I learned you never made a deal with Billy using a contract. You dealt with Billy on a handshake, and Fred Smith of FedEx is the same way. They just come from a different cut of integrity and honesty.

"The first thing I found out about Billy is he was extremely competitive. If you go back to the 1970s when Billy and I would play tennis against each other, we'd have tremendous two and three-set battles.

"He was always damned good and damned competitive. When he owned a home in Maine, I'd go up there in the summer and we'd play on his clay court.

"One day, we were playing there, we were tied at a set and he says, 'Donald, I've got to run inside and make a phone call. I was laughing and said, 'You know, you've only got 10 minutes or you default.' We'd always have bets going.

"So he runs inside, made his phone call and came back out. I said, 'Damn it, you were gone 12, 15 minutes, you're going to be defaulted.' He said, 'I just completed a $2 million cotton sale.' I said, 'What?' He said, 'I had to make a call to China for a $2 million sale.'

"That's the way Billy was. He makes that sale and we go on and finish the third set."

I had to hone my competitive skills against Donald, because the tour stop at The Racquet Club gave me the chance to play exhibitions with and against everybody who had ever been anybody in the tennis world.

Yes, I was nervous when I played the biggest names in tennis. They all beat my ass, but I enjoyed them all – Jimmy Connors, Tony Roche, John Newcombe, Stan Smith, Chris Evert and Martina Navratilova.

They were so good that if any of them didn't want you to win a point, you wouldn't win a point, even as good as you thought you could play.

Chrissie and I won a match together. We played Martina and Pepper Rodgers, who was the head coach of the USFL team I owned in Memphis.

I wasn't thinking about letting them beat us. I don't care if Chrissie played on one leg. I had blood in my eyes. I was going to whip their ass one way or another. It was supposed to go three sets, but we didn't have to play but two.

Pepper was a pretty good player, but he says he recalls being very nervous at the start of that match.

"I'd been in a lot of pressure situations in sports. I'd kicked field goals in bowl games, thrown touchdown passes, coached college teams in tight games. But getting out there in front of 5,000 people and throwing that ball up for the first serve was a lot of pressure. I couldn't raise my arm above my ear.

"As we played, I kept repeating the biggest tactical mistake I ever made in sports. When Martina and I were on defense and I had to lob, I'd lob the ball to Billy when I should have lobbed to Chrissie.

"She would have just hit it back to me, because that's what pros do in those type of matches. But I was stupid enough to keep lobbing to Billy and ol' Billy kept whacking 'em. I got no mercy from Billy."

I met a lot of nice people through tennis, and some unique characters like Bobby Riggs. He was once ranked No. 1 in the world as a pro for a couple of years in the 1940s, winning Wimbledon once and the U.S. Open three times.

But he was best known for challenging Billie Jean King, one of the greatest women players of all-time, to a $100,000 winner-take-all match in the Houston Astrodome in 1973. Bobby lost.

I came across Bobby in an unusual way. I was getting a divorce from my first wife. When I was advised I could get a divorce quicker in Las Vegas where it took just three to six months, I moved to Vegas the very next day.

When I got out there, I lived at The Jockey Club. It had tennis courts. I'd play daily and Herb Flam, the club pro who became one of my buddies, knew I was a pretty good player.

One day, Herb asked me if I wanted to play tennis with Bobby Riggs. It was like jumping over the moon. I said, "Sure, I'd love to." He said, "Come out here tomorrow about 11:30, he'll be out here playing. I'll introduce you to him and y'all can go from there."

The next day, I went out there and Bobby was out there playing against some old fart. Bobby was giving him five games a set and playing him for $1,000 a set. They played three sets, the guy never won a game. Bobby pocketed $3,000.

I knew then he was a hustler. That was his reputation and he never hid behind that. He said, "Yeah, I'll hustle you if I can." He and I got to be buddies.

Right after I got married a second time, he called me. He said, "Billy, Bobby Riggs. I'm in Little Rock for a tennis exhibition. You wanna play?" I said, "Sure, I'd love to play."

Since I owned The Racquet Club. I said, "I'll meet you at The Racquet Club at 11 o'clock tomorrow morning. We'll play."

We meet and I know I'm going to be hustled. But that was OK. He asked me, "How much do you want to play for?" I said, "I'll play you for $100 a set." He says, "Just $100 a set, are you crazy? Let's play for $1,000 a set." I said, "Not me."

So we dickered around and dickered around, but that first day I won $600 to $700 off Bobby. I think it was all a setup, but I did win and he did pay. So we decided to play the next day.

He won the second day and we decided to play a third day. He won the third day. I was still up $350 to $400 on him. I made up my mind he was not going to leave town with my money in his pocket.

We play on and on and on. We finally get down to where we have $100 left of my money that he owes me.

We play one last day. I felt so bad, I had a stomach ache, but I wasn't going to let that stop me. So we played and played and played. I think I ended up winning $50 when Bobby left town.

He was going to Louisville for another exhibition and he told me he'd come back and stay with me for the weekend.

Since I'd just got married again, I told him, "Bobby, there's one thing I don't want to do and that's spend my honeymoon with you." He said, "Well, you might enjoy it more than you think."

Not any money of any consequence ever changed hands until a year later when I went out to Palm Springs where Bobby was playing at the same club I was playing.

We renewed our acquaintances and he won $200 off me. But not any big money, and he always wanted to play for big money. The bigger the better, and I was only half-stupid. I knew I was going to give him some money, but it was worth playing with him just to lose a couple of hundred dollars.

It was a good experience knowing Bobby. He was the kind of guy that if you played him and the ball was just out by a bit, he called it 'in.' He never wanted the reputation of taking somebody. So everything was fair and square with him. He couldn't hustle people if he cheated them. He knew that better than I did. So he never cheated.

The only time I ever lost in tennis intentionally was when we were trying to do business with the country of Uzbekistan and its president Islam Karimov. He was a tough fellow, but he loved to play tennis.

He came down to my Quail Hollow farm in Coffeeville, Mississippi to play doubles. I'll let Steve Ehrhart pick up the story from here.

"This was one of the very few times I played doubles with Billy. I was at the net, Billy was serving, and this guy Karimov was receiving. Billy served and this guy called 'OUT!'

"I look at Billy and said, 'I thought that ball was in.'

Karimov kept calling Billy's serves out, just blatantly cheating. One thing Billy has never tolerated is dishonesty, and this is the only time I saw Billy allow it so he could do business with this guy.

"I looked back at Billy again and said, 'Billy, I can't believe you're allowing him to do this.' Billy said, 'Shut up, Steve.' "

That sumbitch Karimov cheated so bad. A ball could be a foot inside the line and he'd say it was out. I just let it be out, because I wanted his business. We did get the deal done.

Just about every sport I've tried – even badminton, ping-pong and croquet – I've done pretty well. I enjoyed basketball.

But the one sport I wasn't worth a damn in was football. It's ironic that the sport that was my weakness provided some of the most enjoyment I had as an adult when I bought a pro team.

Tennis stars Bjorn Borg (left) and Brian Gottfried played in Billy's National Indoor Tennis Tournament in Memphis.

The Dunavants celebrate Billy's 80th birthday with cowboy legend George Strait, one of Billy's all-time favorite performers.

An oil portrait captures the quiet dignity of Billy's father, William Buchanan Dunavant, a man for all seasons. Even when he was skeet shooting, he was rarely seen without a hat, vest, and necktie.

Recognizing his many contributions to education, in 1985 longtime friend Dr. James Daughdrill, president of Rhodes College, presented Billy with an honorary Doctorate of Humanities.

1985 MEMPH

Top Deck (left to right)

Name	No.
Greg Moser	(84)
Derrick Crawford	(9)
Preston Brown	(81)
Henry Williams	(89)
Gerald Bradley	(80)
Tracy Solem *Assistant Equip. Mgr.*	
Butch Dowty *Assistant Equip. Mgr.*	
Wayne Reed *Equipment Manager*	
Doran Major	(27)
Barney Bussey	(8)
Leonard Coleman	(31)
Don Bessillieu	(47)
John Arnaud	(21)
Tim Spencer	(46)
Ray Odums	(32)
Ron Osborne	(23)
Mike Fox	(29)
Mossy Cade	(3)
Steve Accordino *Film Coordinator*	
Burl Lambert *Assistant Trainer*	
Tony Griffith *Head Trainer*	
Steve Leuze *Assistant Trainer*	
Jim Miller	(1)
Ricky Porter	(26)
Alan Duncan	(7)

Bottom Deck (left to right)

Name	No.
Ken Smith	(61)
Tyrone McGriff	(68)
Carlton Rose	(91)
Steve Hammond	(54)
David Albright	(59)
Will Cokeley	(58)
Larry Rubens	(51)
Russ Bolinger	(73)
Art Kuehn	(50)
Luis Sharpe	(67)
David Huffman	(56)
Jay Hayes	(93)
Reggie White	(92)
John Corker	(53)
Steve Bearden	(99)
Sam Clancy	(90)
John Banaszak	(76)
Daryl Goodlow	(57)
Mike Grant	(55)
Mike Brewington	(52)
Robert Woods	(79)
Calvin Clark	(74)

This poster provided courtesy of Federal Express Corporation

Art Director: David Wade

S SHOWBOATS

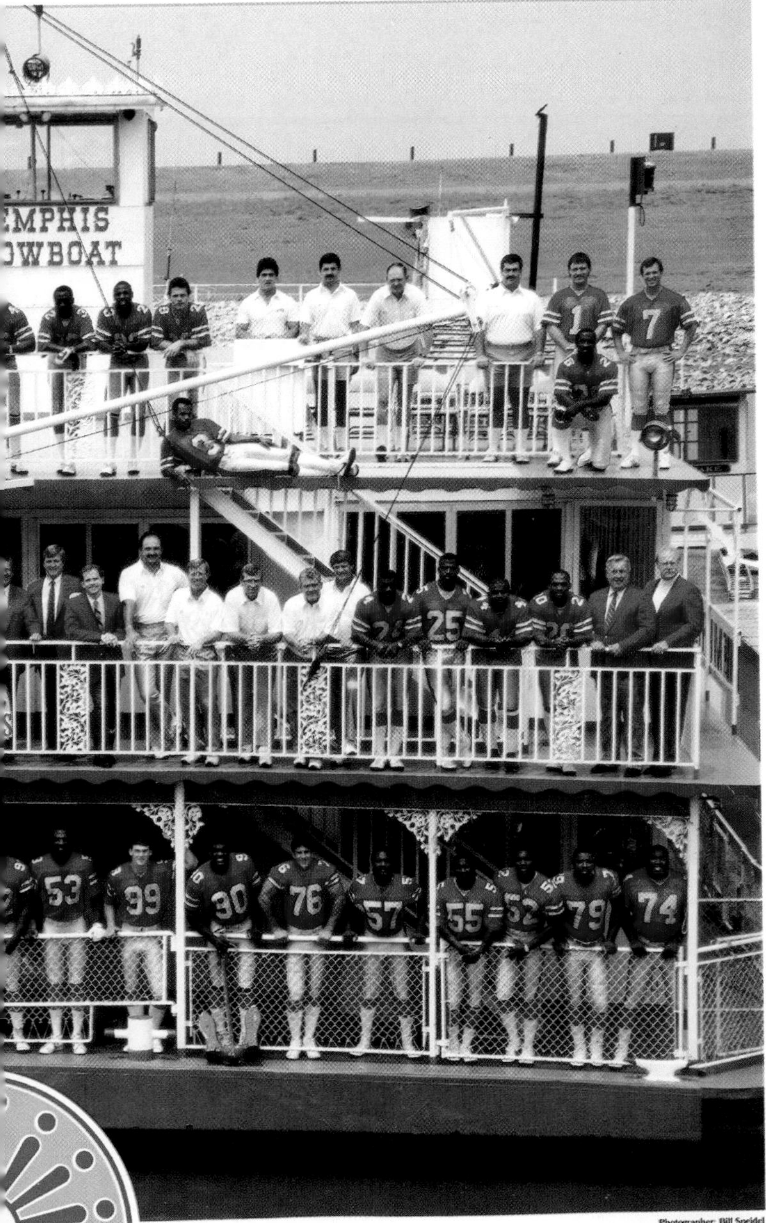

Second Deck
(left to right)
John Griffin
Scout
Gary Shirk (87)
Mark Raugh (83)
Van Heflin (88)
Walter Lewis (10)
Gary Huff (19)
Mike Kelley (12)
Henry Harding
Coach's Assistant
Jimmy Robinson
Receivers Coach
Jairo Penaranda
Special Teams Coach
Ed Emory
Offensive Back Coach
Pepper Rodgers
Head Coach
Rudi Schiffer
V.P., Marketing/ Public Relations
William B. Dunavant, Jr.
Owner
Steve Ehrhart
President and General Manager
Carter Tate
Assistant General Mgr.
Mark Koncar
Asst. Offensive Line Coach
Jimmy Sharpe
Offensive Line Coach
Chuck Dickerson
Defensive Line Coach
Larry Coyer
Linebacker Coach
Bill Oliver
Defensive Back Coach
Harry Sydney (24)
Anthony Parker (25)
Ron O'Neal (44)
Leonard Williams (20)
Bob Patterson
Assistant to the President
Ernie Zwahlen
Scout

MEMPHIS SHOWBOATS™

Photographer: Bill Speidel
FEC Reprographics

OATS™

A relaxing life in "Big Sky" country: the Dunavants' "Crazy D" ranch in Montana.
One of Billy's favorite places to fish is the Sweetgrass
Creek that flows through the ranch.
PHOTOGRAPHS BY KAREN PULFER FOCHT / *THE COMMERCIAL APPEAL* / LANDOV

Billy clearly enjoys the time he spends with Tommie. He has dedicated this book to her: "You have never let me down. You have been there from start to finish, tirelessly working and constantly encouraging me."

PHOTOGRAPH BY KAREN PULFER FOCHT / *THE COMMERCIAL APPEAL* / LANDOV

Billy addresses the crowd at halftime of a Memphis Showboats game at Liberty Bowl Memorial Stadium.

5

Showtime With The Showboats

THE MEMPHIS SHOWBOATS OF THE UNITED States Football League were the favorite of all my sports ownership endeavors. I loved the feeling of camaraderie I had when I owned them.

It wasn't like I was seeking to own a professional team. The USFL, which played a spring and summer schedule, and was never meant to challenge the NFL, started playing in the spring of 1983.

In July of that year, Memphis was awarded a franchise to begin play in 1984, but I originally wasn't a part of it.

The guy who committed to buy the Showboats, Logan Young, never paid for them. Most of his money was tied up in a trust fund. Logan was a nice man and he wasn't a bad person, but he had no more chance of paying for the Showboats than he did swallowing the Goodyear blimp. Once I bought the team, Logan had nothing to do with the franchise except he was a limited partner who had access to a suite upstairs in the Liberty Bowl for home games.

Steve Ehrhart was the USFL's first executive director. He knew what Logan was going through, so he had to find a buyer. Here's how Steve remembers when he first heard my name:

"In 1983, John Bassett and I traveled together putting together the league. He originally owned the Toronto team in the World Football League in the 1970s. But that franchise never got off the

ground because the Canadian government wouldn't allow competition for the Canadian Football League.

"So he moved the Toronto team to Memphis as owner of the original Memphis Southmen/Grizzlies.

"The Grizzlies, a nickname later that stuck with Memphis' NBA franchise in 2001 after it moved from Vancouver, were successful. They had former Dallas Cowboys quarterback Danny White and the Miami Dolphins' Super Bowl trio of Larry Csonka, Jim Kiick and Paul Warfield.

"John also made a big push to bring Memphis to the NFL, but unfortunately at that time Tampa and Seattle got the expansion franchises.

"While John was in Memphis with the WFL team, he and Billy had played tennis together and gotten to know each other.

"Fast forward to 1984, and Billy had emerged in Memphis as a probable USFL owner. Logan Young had put in the expansion application, but when Logan was short on money, I got the word that a guy named Billy Dunavant was going to be the angel that finalized the purchase of the Memphis expansion franchise.

"I didn't know Billy, but everything I needed to know came from John Bassett. He said, 'This is great news. Billy Dunavant is the best guy in the country for our league. He's an aces guy and that's the highest compliment I can give him in all aspects – honor and integrity. He'll be the best guy we'll have in the league.' "

My motivating factor for buying the team was hoping it would be good for Memphis. That was usually my thought process in just about all the athletic endeavors I invested in, because I really didn't make money in any of them.

But I thought they were all worthwhile, from The Racquet Club to the Showboats and even to the Memphis Rockers, a World Basketball League team I co-owned in 1990-91.

Steve Ehrhart was the league commissioner and he got me involved. I'm glad he did because the product was exciting and

I was proud to put together an ownership group featuring five outstanding African-American businessmen from the Memphis area.

Pat Carter, Harold Shaw Jr., George Jones, Claude English and Calvin Anderson joined me to invest in a franchise that featured several former University of Memphis stars and coached by Tom Nissalke, the only man in history to be named Coach of the Year in both the NBA and ABA.

Calvin, who's now senior vice-president and chief of staff for Blue Cross Blue Shield of Tennessee, says as time has passed, being a part of the Rockers' ownership has meant more and more:

"Having known Billy personally and by reputation, it was an honor to be invited into the deal. It was only years later that I recognized the gravity of it.

"Billy didn't need anyone's financial resources to run the team, but he had a vision of being inclusive and having a diverse ownership. He was years ahead of the efforts you now see in ownership diversity in Memphis sports with the Grizzlies.

"It was the only sports-related ownership I've ever had, and to be a basketball fan made it exciting to be part of the ownership group.

"You didn't know how far the franchise could go, but you knew of the love of basketball in Memphis. There were several players on the Rockers and on other teams in the league who went on to play in the NBA.

"When we all sat around the table in owners' meetings, Billy treated us as business partners. What I got to learn from Billy in the two years the franchise existed has been very helpful with other things I've done professionally.

"Billy taught me the importance of being straightforward. The discussions we had as owners and the business planning was very candid.

"Also, I learned the process of decision-making and to have total focus on whatever is in front of me.

"If you're in discussion in a room, there can be a lot of distractions around you. But while you're there, focus on what you need to do now with the issue at hand."

I had no idea whether the Rockers would be successful or not, but I had felt the same way a few years before when I took over the Showboats.

We were able to whip up a lot of enthusiasm in a short period of time with the Showboats, but our first year was a bit rough.

Logan had hired Charlie Thornton, who had been Bear Bryant's public relations man at Alabama, to be our team president and GM. But he left when Logan's deal fell through.

I put the business operations in the hands of H.J. Weathersby, my chief financial officer at Dunavant Enterprises. I left the football side to our coach Pepper Rodgers.

Pepper was a backup quarterback and placekicker when Georgia Tech won the national championship in the early 1950s. He had been a college head coach at Kansas, UCLA and Georgia Tech, but was out of coaching for four seasons before Logan hired him for the Showboats.

Pepper was a fun guy and full of shit, but he could coach. In the beginning, I didn't know much about Pepper and as he recalls, he hardly knew anything about me:

"Since I was a tennis player, the one thing I knew about Billy was he was a very good tennis player that owned The Racquet Club.

"It didn't take long after he bought the Showboats that I learned Billy is extremely, extremely honest. It's kind of hard to say that about anybody, that they don't have a dishonest bone in their body, but he's pretty close. He never told me anything that wasn't straight.

"Billy is also one of the most competitive guys I've ever met, and that was good for our team. To be competitive and have a chance to win, you need good players. I used to tell people I've proved everything a man can prove in coaching. I proved I could win with good players and I proved I couldn't win with bad players.

"Billy always came through. When we needed to get a player we really wanted, Billy was not afraid to spend money and go for it. He would have been a fabulous owner in the National Football League had Memphis gotten a team. He would have been one of the best."

We had a record of 7-11 that first season, and I knew we needed a football and business savvy president/general manager to run our team. I also knew exactly who I wanted – Steve Ehrhart.

Steve had a unique blend of skills. He not only had been an assistant football coach at Colorado and knew the game, but also had a law degree and became an agent that represented more than 100 NFL and NBA players.

I went after the right man, no doubt about it, but a lot of other people were chasing Steve, too, as he recalls:

"Billy had been after me since I came down to a Showboats game in the spring of 1984. We struck it off immediately. He had pride and enthusiasm, and he was competitive. He told me, 'Ehrhart, I'd like you to come down here and be the president and general manager.'

"At that time, I had a contract as the USFL's executive director that ran until that August. I also had another USFL offer from the San Antonio franchise and two or three offers in the NFL.

"Early that summer, Billy flew my wife Mary and me to Memphis so we could go to his Quail Hollow farm in Coffeeville to talk about the job. He put me in a car with his second wife Ann, and he took Mary in his car for the 90-minute drive. The reason he

The Memphis Showboats management in 1984 (l-r): head coach Pepper Rodgers, owner Billy Dunavant, and president/general manager Steve Ehrhart.

put Mary in his car was for him to connect with her. To this day, they have an unbelievably close connection that started in that car ride.

"That was an amazing day at the farm. That was the man in his passion and in his arena. He created it. He took me in his truck and drove all over his property. As we bounced across fields, through thickets and between trees, we talked about his love for fishing and hunting.

"Finally, Billy gets me in a boat in the middle of the lake. We're fishing and I was casting and getting snagged. He was being very patient unsnagging me, something he wouldn't normally do for anybody else. I learned later that he was not a patient fisherman.

"He said, 'I appreciate that you had the integrity not to break your word to the league. That's the kind of man I want for this franchise.'

"So we crafted a deal sitting in that boat for me to leave my job with the USFL and come to Memphis as the Showboats' president/general manager and receive five percent of team ownership. Billy made a Godfather deal, an offer I couldn't refuse. Plus, he wasn't going to let me out of the boat until I said yes.

"We shook hands and I said, 'Now take me back to shore.' He wasn't going to let me out of that boat until I shook his hand to cement the deal.

"That's why we have been so close for all these years. His reputation is about honor and integrity. I've stuck with Billy for 30 years and I'd jump off a cliff or run through a wall for him. His word is his bond, and he instilled that in me.

"Late that summer when we moved to Memphis, Billy hosted a welcome party at his home. He invited key people from the community to give me the opportunity to connect. He did everything right. The one thing I learned from Billy is he does everything in a first-class way. He's taught everybody around him to do that. You treat people in a first-class way. That's the transcendent aura about him.

"With the Showboats, we ran the team in a first-class, NFL-style manner. We were building the team to be the best, whether it was in the USFL or leading to the NFL.

"Billy said, 'Build a championship team here in Memphis and do what you gotta do. We want to do as well financially as we can, but get some really good players.'

"We had five No. 1 NFL draft choices on our team — Reggie White, Tim Spencer, Mossy Cade, Leonard Coleman, and Luis Sharpe — but all chose to sign with us. We had a lot of vets, like Sam Clancy who later played for the Browns and the Colts. In 1990, five years after the USFL ended, there were still 17 Memphis Showboats playing in the NFL.

"The first year I was in Memphis, which also turned out to be the last year of our league, we made quite a few personnel changes.

We flipped that 7-11 record from the year before to 11-7, advancing to the league semifinals before we lost to the Oakland Invaders.

"One of my great memories of Billy that season came in the locker room after we beat the league's defending champ, the Baltimore Stars, on the road. Billy, so full of excitement and energy wearing a Showboats red jacket, got up on a chair and said, 'I'm so proud of you guys. I want to invite all of you to come down to my farm in Coffeeville for a day of celebration and fun.'

"The whole locker room explodes. How many owners would invite all the coaches, support staff, 50 players and their spouses to a day at his home? A couple of days later, he had this huge cookout. Have you ever seen 300-pound guys drive jet skis or boats? Billy just turned them loose. It was like an adult Disneyland.

"Billy taught me a few things that first year, like you'd better be prepared to fight if you call people rednecks in the South.

"The Showboats were playing at Birmingham and we were in a press box booth next to the Birmingham coaches. They were screaming and pounding the booth every time they did something well, and we were smoldering a bit because we thought there were some questionable penalties against Reggie White.

"We left our box about the same time as the coaches and Billy tells them, 'Keep it down, you rednecks.' I didn't realize 'rednecks' was fighting words in the South.

"A couple of these young coaches wanted to fight Billy. He said, 'Bring it on.' They backed off.

"We had a great run that season. The city appreciated the Showboats like nothing else. It was front-page news. People to this day love the Showboats. We brought in great players and we connected with the community. Billy set the first-class tone."

Once I got into owning a team, it was a dream. I got the fever so bad it was embarrassing. I would have hated to take my blood pressure on gamedays. I guarantee you it was high.

We had quality players and people like the late Reggie White, who became a Pro Football Hall of Famer. He left this life way too early. He died a day after Christmas at age 43 from a heart problem. He was a good, good man who could do impressions and laugh at himself. Pepper Rodgers remembers the time Reggie went clothes shopping as a rookie and naively bought hundreds of dollars worth of socks from a persuasive salesman.

"Reggie was upset because the media had gotten wind of the socks shopping spree. I told Reggie and the team, 'Here's how we'll fix it. When each of you is introduced before Saturday's home game, you're going to run out on the field waving a sock. Reggie is going to be the last player introduced and he's going to come running out with a bunch of socks in each hand. Then he's going to run around the stadium throwing socks into the stands. I said, 'Reggie, they've poked fun at me all my life, but they can't get to me because I don't take myself that seriously. I take my job seriously, but not myself.'

"Ol' Reggie ran around the field throwing the socks, and then he wrote about it later in some religious magazine. My mother was so proud, because I'd never gotten written up in any religious magazine."

I loved Reggie so much that we did everything we could to get him to the NFL once the Philadelphia Eagles showed some interest. But as Steve Ehrhart remembers, Eagles' owner Norman Braman was sort of arrogant when we met with him about Reggie:

"The principal owner of the Philadelphia Eagles, Norman Braman calls me. He says, 'My guys tell me you got a player we're interested in.'

"Pete Rozelle had barred any owners from talking to the USFL because we were in the middle of a lawsuit. But Braman said, 'I don't give a damn. I'll fly down there and meet with you guys.'

"Braman flies to Memphis, I take him to Mr. Dunavant's office and he starts going on about how he'd be doing us a favor to give Reggie an opportunity to play in the NFL.

"Billy and I are looking at each other, and getting more and more pissed off. The thing that finally sent me over the edge is Braman says, 'He (White) might be able to make our team and you're holding him back by having him play for the Memphis Showboats.'

"I look at Billy and Billy gives me the nod to 'go ahead.' I was respectful. I said, 'Mr. Braman, he's not only better than anybody you've got on your whole team, he may be better than anybody in the whole damned NFL.'

"Braman gets up angry. Billy says, 'Mr. Braman, I think this conversation is over with.'

"I take Braman back to the airport and he didn't understand how good Reggie was. I told him we'd had Reggie two years and he's not only a great leader, his teammates love him. He's one of the most athletically blessed 300-pound athletes I'd ever seen.

"The Eagles bribed Reggie's agent and said they'd get him a job if he delivered Reggie. They got in his ear about how he should play for the Eagles. Reggie started calling us. Finally, Billy said, 'Let's do what we can to help him out.'

"When Reggie found out what the Eagles had done, he fired that agent and he hired his suitemate from Tennessee named Jimmy Sexton. That's how Jimmy Sexton, who's now one of the most powerful sports agents in the nation, got his start.

"When Reggie finally joined the Eagles without any training camp, he had three sacks in his first game. He had 13 sacks his first year, played 15 years in the NFL, had 198 sacks, won a Super Bowl ring with Green Bay and became one of the league's most popular players.

Reggie White — "The Minister of Defense" — was the Memphis Showboats MVP and a pro football Hall-of-Famer.

"To Reggie's credit, he later came back and saw Billy. They resolved every thing. His wife Sarah said when Reggie was inducted into the Pro Football Hall of Fame that he enjoyed his years with the Showboats.

"Reggie loved Billy so much he came back to Memphis and did speaking engagements in Memphis, especially for the Boy Scouts which is one of Billy's passions. Every time he saw Billy, he never failed to give him his Reggie White bearhug."

Another player on the Showboats I respected was Walter Lewis. He was one of our quarterbacks and the first African-American to start as QB for the University of Alabama. He still keeps in contact with me. He lives in Birmingham and is a managing partner of a venture capital company. He's a fabulous guy, very bright and I sure respect him. In fact, we had dinner together in Memphis just after I started writing this book and he says it was as good a night for him as it was for us:

"That dinner with Billy and his wife Tommie was the first time since I left Memphis in the 1980s that I saw Billy in person. We've had some phone conversations over the years.

"When I call Billy from time to time, I never really talk business. I call just to stay in touch and see how's he doing, because I appreciate him as a man. I appreciate the leadership qualities he possesses.

"I often reflect back about people such as Billy that have had an impact on my life.

"When we crossed paths when I played for the Showboats and he owned them, I didn't know Billy personally. I observed him from a distance, and you can pick up vibes how that person is. Billy has had a strategic impact on me in terms of how I see things in life and in business as well.

"Billy came into a distraught situation when he took the Showboats from the previous owner. Before he got involved, our team

had no vision. As soon as he got involved, he cast a vision of where he wanted us to go. He was very succinct, he was very direct and the type of guy that when he put his hand into something he was in it 110 percent.

"He had expectations and a passion about competing and wanting to win, about putting the right people in the right places in order to get that done. All that carried over to the team from the top to the bottom.

"The time he invited the whole team to his farm in Mississippi spoke volumes. That day everybody became enamored with Billy. Because when you can impart yourself to someone outside the profession you're in, it shows a semblance of caring for those who are working for you.

"Those are unique qualities that people gravitate to, and to me that's one of the reasons Billy has been so successful, why he has been so respected in the Memphis community. He wanted everybody involved – the city, his family, the team members, his company – and that's just special.

"If you go back to the Biblical days, there are a lot of analogies that identify with Billy Dunavant, like in the book of Moses. Moses is in the Pharaoh's Court and he was a rich guy. But Moses saw his people were suffering. He left Pharaoh's Court and joined his people where he could really get a feel for how he could help them.

"Billy was that way. He didn't circle on his high horse on his mountain of wealth. He actually came into the valley where common people worked. Those are great leadership qualities.

"I played for Coach (Bear) Bryant at Alabama, but I never sat down with Coach Bryant and just talked about life. It wasn't that type of a relationship.

"When I had dinner with Billy and Tommie, I saw him not as the past owner of the Showboats or someone above me, I saw him eye-to-eye as a man. That was a great moment for me just to sit

A sell-out crowd fills the Liberty Bowl during the June 16, 1984, matchup between the Memphis Showboats and the Birmingham Stallions.

down with them and chat about things past, present and future. To me, that's what it's all about."

We had some pretty good talent on the Showboats. If our league hadn't tried to sue the NFL for the right to play in the fall by filing an antitrust suit claiming the NFL had a monopoly on TV rights and access to playing venues, we would have hung in three or four more years. The league could have worked a little longer if it had stayed in the spring, but the lawsuit put us out of business.

We had one team owner who was the mouth of the league, pushing the lawsuit. He wanted to do things his way, and because of it the league folded.

That owner was Donald Trump of the New Jersey Generals. Yes, that Donald Trump. I know him well and in my opinion he's a true jerk.

He thought the USFL was better than the NFL. That's how pompous and conceited he is. He loved to talk down to people, just loved it. If you didn't have what he had, you wouldn't get the time of day from him.

No question he ruined the league. He was arrogant then, he's arrogant now and he'll probably always be arrogant.

I was one of the few owners that paid his bills promptly. That was the only thing Donald liked about me. When I told him I would do something, I did it. He respected that, but I thought he didn't like me personally.

You had to shame him into doing anything concerning money. That's just Donald's background, getting something for nothing. If you had to sit in one meeting with Donald Trump, it would ruin your day.

After the USFL, I never thought I'd get in football again.

But when a Memphis ownership group was put together in 1993 to chase an NFL expansion franchise, and it involved such partners as Fred Smith who founded FedEx, Pitt Hyde who started AutoZone, my cousin Paul Tudor Jones who's one of the world's best money managers and Elvis Presley Enterprises, I was all in again.

Billy Dunavant led the effort to bring the NFL to Memphis.

6

Flirting With The NFL

When the NFL began looking to expand in the early 1990s, I definitely wanted a team for Memphis.

Owning an NFL franchise wouldn't have been good for me. In fact, the stress from becoming so emotionally involved because I'm such a competitor would have killed me. But it would have been good for Memphis, and that's all that mattered to me.

Our ownership group was strong as anybody in the NFL. Besides me, we had FedEx founder Fred Smith, AutoZone founder Pitt Hyde, my cousin Paul Tudor Jones, Willard Sparks, Pro Football Hall of Famer Willie Davis, Elvis Presley Enterprises, Mike Starnes, and Steve Ehrhart.

We jumped through a lot of hoops, but we missed the big hoop. We didn't build a new stadium, and that was it in a nutshell. Charlotte and Jacksonville were awarded the expansion franchises.

Without a new stadium, a monkey had a better chance of getting an NFL team than we did. We were so naïve. We believed we could still overcome that.

But it was frustrating. My friend John Dobbs remembers hearing me on the phone with NFL commissioner Paul Tagliabue when we were on a hunting trip in England:

"I walked in the bedroom and Billy said, 'I'm on the phone with Tagliabue.' He talks and talks. He tells Tagliabue, 'Tagliabue, I'm withdrawing, I'm not going to try to get a franchise anymore.'

Cousins Billy Dunavant and Paul Tudor Jones were the managing partners of the NFL effort.

Tagliabue said, 'Billy, you're making a mistake. There's two franchises left. We have nobody left in the Central time zone. We definitely aren't giving one to St. Louis. We've already given one to Charlotte. It's between you and Jacksonville. Jacksonville is the Eastern time zone and we need a Central time zone franchise.' He said, 'Okay, I'll hang in there for another couple million.' He did and guess what? They screwed him. They used him."

We tried as hard as we could. But all the NFL could talk about was our stadium, Liberty Bowl Stadium, which was almost 30 years old. Pepper Rodgers, our Showboats' coach, stayed on board as a consultant as we pursued an NFL franchise.

Pepper helped promote several NFL exhibitions that we hosted to prove to the NFL we were worthy of a franchise. He was one of the most upbeat and optimistic people I've ever met, yet he pessimistically recalls one of the NFL's visits to Memphis during our quest for a team:

"I rode around Memphis with current NFL commissioner Roger Goodell, when he served as an officer for the league. I drove him around to show we had a city large enough to support a team.

"All he talked about was the stadium.

"I couldn't blame him. I was an assistant coach at UCLA under Tommy Prothro, a Memphis guy, and we played Tennessee during the regular season in 1965 in Liberty Bowl Stadium. So here we are almost 30 years later trying to get an NFL team by simply adding skyboxes.

"That would have been like me going through a weight and running program, becoming a rock and running as fast as I could. But I still wouldn't be as good as I was 30 years ago.

"It was almost a three decades old stadium and we tried to doll it up. Jacksonville, who didn't have the number of TV sets we did, tore down its stadium, built a new one and it got an NFL team.

"Memphis eventually got an NBA team and built a new arena for it. But we always believed the NFL would have worked better in Memphis than the NBA, because it's so much easier to get them to fill up a stadium for eight home games a year than it is for 41 home games in the NBA. You'd draw from a wider area, from middle and East Tennessee, south to Jackson, Mississippi, west to Little Rock, maybe north into Missouri and southeast into Alabama. Because we saw people in Memphis who'd drive 300 miles to Knoxville for University of Tennessee home games, we felt a Memphis NFL franchise would have been a regional team."

I can certainly say that our ownership group did its due diligence. Everyone had roles in pursuing the franchise, and everybody was relentless. Fred Smith, who now owns part of the Washington Redskins, has an excellent recollection of how our chase for a franchise played out:

"My job, as part of our ownership group, was combining FedEx business trips with visits to see NFL owners like Leon Hess with the Jets, Lamar Hunt with the Chiefs and others.

"It quickly became apparent they had a lot of respect for Billy, and they knew he wasn't a rabblerouser in USFL litigation. They'd look at us on an even basis.

"We had a fabulous ownership group, with Billy right in the middle of it as the majority owner. We had the best ownership group with the exception of Jerry Richardson in Charlotte.

"St. Louis and Baltimore, cities that had previously lost teams – St. Louis to Phoenix and Baltimore to Indianapolis – had competing ownership groups seeking teams. They got into litigation once against each other. They were given teams that moved from California and Cleveland.

"There was a great sentiment from other owners that those cities should get a team back. But there were a lot of people in the NFL that said, 'Look, they didn't support a team they had. Why should they get a second bite of the apple?'

"Then, you had Memphis and Charlotte with a good owner in a good market seeking expansion franchises. Jacksonville was really out of the picture until Wayne Weaver, who was in the shoe business in Connecticut as owner of the Shoe Carnival and Nine West chains, became a potential owner.

"Unlike Memphis, Jacksonville had a very aggressive mayor and they had a newspaper, The Times-Union, *that was hugely supportive of the effort. In fact, the newspaper gave the NFL effort a floor in the newspaper's office building to promote the effort to build a new stadium. Jacksonville's offer was it would take the Gator Bowl down to the foundation and build a new stadium.*

"At the end of the day, our ownership group was probably too cautious. Other cities were more aggressive in the terms of what

they were offering, such as some of our proposals to pay the visiting teams. You go through this period of time before you are fully in the club that you pay the other teams. So maybe we were light on that.

"But the biggest single fundamental reason we didn't get the franchise, and I don't think anybody has ever said this, was Lionel Linder getting killed.

"Lionel was the editor of The Commercial Appeal, *our daily newspaper in Memphis. He was sort of a Chamber of Commerce guy. He was absolutely in support of Memphis getting an NFL team, which he felt, we felt and most people felt would be a transformation for the city.*

"Willie Herenton had just become mayor in Memphis and he was very cautious about doing things that would be criticized by the community, particularly by the newspaper.

"Lionel was tragically killed on New Year's Eve 1992 driving home on Union Avenue. A driver charged with a DUI crossed the road and hit Lionel's car.

"When Lionel died, I was a member of the board of Scripps Howard, the media company that owned The Commercial Appeal. *We brought in Angus McEachran to replace Lionel.*

"Angus was a very different guy than Lionel. I'm not saying he was a bad guy or good guy, but he wasn't that Chamber of Commerce guy. Angus was an old hardline newspaper guy, just the facts, and he didn't think it was the newspaper's job to promote any particular business. He wasn't against it, but he just wasn't the cheerleader for it.

"So Pepper Rodgers and I went to see Roger Goodell, and Roger Goodell made it crystal clear – no new stadium, no chance to get an NFL franchise, period.

"Willie Herenton, without the backing of The Commercial Appeal, *wouldn't get out front and say, 'We need to build a new stadium and issue bonds.' He wasn't in the job long enough.*

"Everybody knows the story about Bud Adams and the Houston Oilers. He just gave Nashville the damned team. To prove my point about how important the stadium and political leadership is, then-Nashville mayor Phil Bredesen told Bud Adams, 'We'll build you a new stadium, we'll issue the bonds and we want you here.' So Nashville got the Oilers, now the Titans.

"As Memphis subsequently showed, it built the FedExForum to attract an NBA team. It has been fabulous and the Grizzlies have been a good consolation prize. That just showed what we could have done. It could have been the NFL before the NBA, but we were not willing to build a new stadium.

"Memphis was a better media market than Jacksonville, it was a Central time zone market, it was just better in every respect save one – we would not build a new stadium, so the Memphis Jaguars are the Jacksonville Jaguars.

"Look at Jacksonville now, and it has both ends of its stadium covered by tarps. It was very successful initially but the demographics of Jacksonville vs. the demographics of Memphis and the Mid-South doesn't compare. With fewer home games than the NBA and a fan base extending to surrounding states, we could have definitely filled up an NFL stadium eight times a year in the regular season, preseason and playoffs.

"It was a great missed opportunity. Billy would have been an outstanding owner. As competitive as he is, just by force of will, it's astounding we didn't get that NFL team."

Fred Smith is the person who really needs to be the majority owner of a sports team. He really wants to and he will with the right situation. By far, he's a football guy.

We don't do a lot of socializing together because neither of us likes to socialize. But he's a close friend. He's a wonderful man. If he likes you, he'll literally do anything for you. When I call him, he always calls me right back.

The day it was announced that Jacksonville had gotten the expansion franchise, I already knew my next move. Now that I wasn't going to buy an NFL franchise, that money could go to buying something Tommie and I had discussed for a while:

"Billy said, 'Tommie, if we don't get a team, we're going straight from the (owners) meeting. We're going to go out West and find a place.' We had people looking in Colorado and in Wyoming.

"One thing Billy taught me is that when something happens in life and you can't do anything about it, when the curtain comes down, you shake the dust from under your feet and move on. There's no need to sit there spinning.

"So we left the owners meeting after they voted for Jacksonville. We went straight to the airport, got on Billy's plane and went straight to Montana to buy a ranch."

The big Montana sky spills into Billy's office at "Crazy D" in Big Timber.

PHOTOGRAPH BY KAREN PULFER FOCHT / *THE COMMERCIAL APPEAL* / LANDOV

7

Life Under The Blue Clear Sky

WELCOME TO OUR RANCH 25 MILES FROM Big Timber, Montana, where we live several months a year in a house that we built 19 years ago.

Yes, I'm "D" and I'm crazy, so we call our ranch "Crazy D." And also crazy for the Crazy Mountains, which along with the Absarokas and the Bear Tooth, are three mountain ranges that surround us.

I'll live longer because of the ranch, no question. Probably been dead now if I had owned an NFL team. Things happen for a reason.

Now, hop in the truck with our dog Simba and me. We're going to tour the property that covers about 12,500 acres.

But before we start, I'm going to get Roy Sims to tell you how he found the Crazy D. Roy has probably lived in 12 states and managed Dunavant Enterprise properties, like our Montana property, for nine years. They were all farm properties. Some of them could be developed and were developed into commercial real estate. We'd fix them up and re-sell them.

I always pledged that if I didn't buy a football team that I was going to find a ranch. Roy spent a lot of hours out here looking and he found lots of ranches. I knew he'd find us a good property here as he recalls:

"Billy told me, find me a ranch in Montana. I looked for more than a year in Idaho, Colorado, Wyoming and Montana. I called every realtor looking at pieces of property all over and finally ended up with this one near Big Timber. There was one in Red Rock that was 10,000 acres at 9,000 feet elevation.

"But this one had lots of wildlife and wading streams with bigger fish. And it's one of the best ranches for its size."

We're going to drive down the road and find the house on our ranch that we originally bought and lived in for almost three years while the house we have now was being built.

Here it is.

It's really a nice, big house. We had some good experiences here. You can see we were right on the creek. We bought it from the Starrs. Tommie remembers the sale being extremely emotional for Mrs. Starr, who had lived in the house for almost 30 years:

"We looked at several places and this one was great. Billy had been told that Mr. Starr was a man of his word. He was selling the property but didn't want to negotiate. What he wanted was what he wanted, and if he said it, it was yours.

"So we're having lunch with the Starrs at their house. Billy leans over and says, 'Well, Norm, I'll take it.' Norm stuck out his hand and like Billy, all you needed with this man was a handshake.

"All of sudden, the wife starts crying softly. Norm says, 'Now Lorraine, we've had this discussion.' She says, 'But I didn't know anybody would buy it this soon.' He says, 'Well, they have.'

"Billy and Norm are down at one end of the table talking like long-lost buddies. Every time Lorraine passes me she cries.

"So lunch is over and Norm says to Lorraine, 'You need to show Tommie the house.' She says, 'My house?' He says, 'Yes, Lorraine, because it's going to be HER house.'

Bringing the great outdoors inside — the rustic interior of the main house at the "Crazy D" Ranch in Montana.

"So we start through the house and she starts, 'This is my daughter's bedroom.' I say, 'Lorraine, that's all right. I don't need to see that.'

"I felt like the biggest homewrecker. It might have seemed weird that we bought it immediately, but we'd prayed about it and we knew it was the right place."

See how the creek runs next to the bedroom? We would have been fine living here for a long time, but our plan was to build a house where we could see the lake, the creek and the mountains.

Tommie and I drove every day for two weeks and looked for just the right spot to build the house. I don't think we could have picked any better spot on this piece of property.

A guy from Bozeman designed our house. He'd never done anything like this. I just looked him up, told him what Tommie and I wanted. He drew some plans, negotiated and got them approved.

For us, the Crazy D is perfect. I love to hunt and I love to fish, and this offers all of that. Our duck and goose hunting is spectacular in October and November, and we hunt deer. But it gets so windy out here that you have to tie your deer stands down with wire. If you don't, that wind will blow that son-of-a-gun into another county.

This stream right here is Sweetgrass Creek. It's got lots of brown trout in it, very few rainbows. Right now, I can cross it. A week ago, the current was heavy. We fish Sweetgrass Creek by wading through it.

Look way over there and you can see that big bluff called the buffalo jump. It's where the Indians would take the buffalo, run them off the jump, and they'd all fall to the bottom. The Indians would go down to the bottom of the jump and slaughter the buffalos because they would be crippled or killed. Buffalo is a good eating piece of meat.

You'll see a little bit of everything on the Crazy D. We've got antelope, duck, geese, whitetail deer, mule deer, elk, moose, bears, mountain lions, skunks and a fair amount of golden eagles and bald eagles that start migrating here in late September. We have lots of porcupines in the fall and they are a pain in the ass.

These are our beehives. They do all the pollinating of the grasses. We collect our honey. In October somebody picks up the hives and takes them to California where the bees work there in the winter.

We cut a lot of these fields for hay, and that light green stuff through there is barley. We'll harvest that the last week of August, and then I'll run ducks in those fields.

That red place in the distance is a hanger of the airplane of George Cremer, who owns 80,000 acres next to ours. A plane is the best way for him to see all his property. We have lots of fire problems out here and with all that acreage he has to really stay on top of it.

We hired Dan Groshens, a conservationist who lives nearby in Big Timber. Before I bought the Starrs' house, I had a house in Livingston. I used a fly shop named George Anderson's and I met Dan through George Anderson's.

Dan started as a hunting and fishing guide for me. But as he'll tell you, he quickly became much more than that:

"I was very dubious working for Billy at first. The longest job I held before I came here was four or five years. February 2015 marked 20 years working for Billy.

"He hired me, we went through some negotiations and he said, 'If you're still working for me 10 years from now you'll be making X amount of dollars.' He was true to his word. He gave me a raise every year and has continued to treat my family and me well.

"Billy is very generous, he's a man of his word. He says he's going to do something, and he does it. When I first started working for him, I was just doing the hunting and fishing part. Now, I'm taking care of all the houses.

"I became the caretaker because the guy they had quit. That happened after less than a month after they first sodded the lawn around the new house, right after construction was completed.

"With the house finished, Billy and Tommie moved in and went back to Memphis. It was the middle of the summer, and the sod was still being irrigated to keep it green. Somebody left the gate open, they moved some cattle down in this field, cows came up here, walked around the outside of the house and completely destroyed the sod.

The next morning, the caretaker came, saw the torn-up sod and said, 'I quit.'

It's a long way from Cotton Row — "Owning this ranch feeds my soul."

"Billy had nobody to take care of his main house, and the six other houses on the property. My background was in carpentry and building, and I said, 'I can be the caretaker but you're going to have to pay me for it, it's going to enlarge my job description.' He said, 'Whatever you want just go ahead and do it.'

"Taking care of the main house is a lot of work, as well as the other houses. I take care of all of them and still do the hunting and fishing with him.

"I've been fired by Billy at least a half dozen times, but the next day it was like it never happened.

"I'm the opposite. When somebody says that to me, I think, 'That's it.' The first time he fired me, and the next day it was like nothing ever happened.

"He said, 'I'm going to fire you. You've really screwed up.' The next day, he's like, 'Where are we going to fish today?' I was ex-

pecting to have to move my family out of the house. He was like, 'Forget about that. Just don't let it happen again.'

"After about 10 years, you get used to that."

Tommie and I and the dogs will ride around the property about 9:30 every morning. We'll make notes and comments about what needs or doesn't need to be done.

Sometimes, you don't know what you'll see, as Tommie explains:

"You see everything here, including a boxing goat. Yes, I said boxing goat.

"There was a Mexican woman named Louisa whose husband worked on our ranch and she worked in our house. She was always saving something and she found this goat on the side of the road where somebody left it to die.

"She fed it cat food because this old goat had no teeth. She and her family lived in a house on our ranch, and Billy gave her permission to keep the goat. She named the goat 'Billy.'

"Whenever my Billy would go down to the house and walk in the yard, Billy the Goat would come out, stand up on his back legs and box with Billy. They'd dance around the yard and throw play punches."

Maybe they were play punches from me, but that goat had a good right jab. He loved to box. Soon as I got out of the truck, he'd stand up and come after me.

There were also the times we'd walk around the lake near our house almost every day. It's a nice, long walk since it's 7½ miles around.

One day, we were on our normal walk when a pheasant starting walking with us. I'll let Tommie pick up the story:

"This pheasant would walk a whole section of the lake with us. When we stopped, he stopped. He'd come up to Billy and kind of pounce at his feet.

"This went on for several days. I named him Peter. We could walk, call him and he'd fly. If we went in the truck, we'd call him and he'd land on the truck.

"Peter liked Billy. We had Montana, a German shepherd at that time. Peter would land on the window, lean in and peck Montana on the nose.

"One day we go riding down here, and there's snow. In the middle of the road is a dead pheasant, breast up, because the eagles eat them. I start crying, I'm hysterical, because I'm certain an eagle has killed Peter.

"Billy gets out and he's holding the carcass of a dead pheasant. He says, 'Don't cry, Tommie. This isn't Peter. His tail isn't long enough. This is some other old pheasant. This isn't Peter.'

"About that time, Peter lands at Billy's feet. He'd ride with us to down here on the truck and then he'd fly back.

"We're getting ready to go home for the winter. Billy says, 'I don't want anything to happen to Peter.' So he talks Dan into capturing Peter in a trap. We talked to the people down the road that had a farm and raised pheasant. We asked them if they'd take Peter from us for the winter and when we came back in the summer they'd give Peter back to us. Billy was paying them astronomical money to keep our Peter.

"One day in the middle of the winter, Dan gets a phone call. Some deer have run through a field, they knocked the fence down and Peter is gone.

"So Dan and his kids go out riding down roads calling Peter's name. About the time Dan said he was feeling pretty stupid riding through snow calling the name of a pheasant, Peter lands on the back of the truck. They re-capture him and we released him when we came back on our next trip. We never saw Peter again.

"Sophie Coors heard this story. She was so touched by it that a month before she died she painted a wonderful picture of Billy and Peter.

"John Sartelle, one of Billy's friends, said Peter was one of the smartest pheasants he ever knew. He said Peter made friends with his worst enemy, because Billy pheasant hunts. Every time Billy would go to shoot, he would look to make sure he wasn't Peter."

We've got a place in Texas that's really nice, but not built as well as the Crazy D. For us, it's the location and the pace of life is perfect.

We have solitude, but usually one night a week we'll venture into Big Timber for dinner at the Grand Hotel. It has a superb chef named Amy Smith. She makes it worth the short drive.

I always had a dream to own something in the West. For us, Montana is perfect. Owning this ranch feeds my soul.

Billy with his first hunting dog, Chief, on a duck hunting expedition.

8

The Great Outdoors

I WAS A VERY OUTDOORSY YOUNG MAN. IT DIDN'T matter if it was playing sports, hunting and fishing, I lived outdoors.

Both my parents loved the outdoors. Daddy loved to hunt and fish, and Momma loved to fish. So it was a nice experience for us to be able to do those things together.

Just about every Saturday and Sunday, we would go fishing as a family and in hunting season we would go hunting. For about 15 years, my dad was president of a hunting and fishing club called Hatchie Coon in Trumann, Arkansas, and then when he stepped down I became president.

Because we enjoyed the outdoors as a family, I know it influenced me to start my annual father/son hunt that I host every September at my Quail Hollow property in Coffeeville, Mississippi.

I started it 60 years ago when I was in my 20s and always on the second weekend of dove season. Over the years, it has progressed from father/son to father/son/grandson/great grandsons. The fact it has been generational means a great deal to me. I think my parents would have been proud that friends like Steve Ehrhart understand that connection:

"The father-son hunt has impacted so many lives, like the time I've spent at those hunts with my son Ryan. Billy knows I'm the worst hunter in the world ever, but he gave the inspiration to Ryan to become an avid hunter. He's obsessed with it and he understands the conservation of the land."

Billy with a prize Atlantic salmon taken on the Moisie River in Quebec, Canada.

I've been fortunate that I've been able to fish and hunt just about anywhere in the world, from Mississippi to Iceland, from Texas to Spain, from Montana to Cuba, from Maine to England.

I've always kept diaries, large leather-bound books, and recorded every hunt I've been on. I write down where I hunted, what I hunted, the weather conditions and how I did. If I did badly, I said I did. I didn't lie.

When I mean everything is in these diaries, I mean everything. Tommie knows what do with them when I die:

"Billy told me to burn them. He doesn't want them to fall in the hands of a game warden."

I've hunted just about everything. Ducks, turkeys, pheasants, deer, lions, leopards and buffalo. I've learned to hunt them all and I've killed them all. I've been on two safaris to Africa. I never shot an elephant because it's not sporting.

I've had everything mounted and they are in my African room on the top floor of our ranch house in Montana. I hunted big game to say that I did it, but I don't do that anymore. I don't think much was accomplished doing that.

I'm really more of a birdman when it comes to hunting, because it's simply more challenging.

There were a few times in the past when I've been arrested for a game violation, but I've never been convicted. I'd admitted to some violations because it was easier to pay the fine than go to court.

There was a time in Mississippi that I was caught by a game warden when not only was I duck hunting out of season but I was way over the limit. The game warden liked me and I liked him, so we came up with the idea of me awarding a conservation scholarship at Mississippi State. I gave that out for four years, which I thought covered the penalty for the violations.

Now that doesn't mean I still don't like a homefield advantage every now and then, like my longtime friend Eli Tullis remembers:

"We were duck hunting at Billy's camp at Mallard Rest. We got there early before the sun came up. When it got daylight, I looked down at the bottom of the pond and it was glistening gold.

"I said, 'Billy, what in the hell do you have down there?' He said, 'Two tons of corn.' I couldn't believe it. I said, 'Oh, my God, we're going to jail for baiting, for violating the law of migratory birds.'

"Billy is the longest and fastest shot I've ever seen. One time I was with him, he had a gun in the tree with six shells and he had a gun in his hand with six shells. Birds were coming, but I didn't shoot because I wanted to see what Billy could do.

"The birds come across us around the willows. BAM, BAM, BAM, BAM, BAM, BAM! He drops that gun in the water, grabs the other gun. BAM, BAM, BAM, BAM, BAM, BAM! He killed 10 and wounded the 12th. That was the damndest shooting I ever saw."

My dogs have always been trained to respond to my multiple gunshots. As my longtime business partner Sam Reeves recalls, my dogs don't particularly care retrieving for anybody who isn't as good a shot as me:

"Sometimes Billy would put me in one of his duck blinds by myself, and you always had one or two of his dogs who were trained to run and retrieve as soon as that shotgun was fired. The gun would go off, those dogs would jump into freezing ice water because they knew there was a duck or were multiple ducks shot by Billy.

"I'm in the blind by myself, my gun goes off and the dog hits the water. God forbid you didn't get a duck, because if you didn't that dog would come back to the blind irate. He'd stand next to you and shake off all that cold water on you. The dog was so pissed I didn't get a duck he'd take it out on me.

"If you are in the same duck blind with Billy, he'll say 'Stay down, stay down, stay down,' and all of sudden BOOM BOOM BOOM BOOM BOOM BOOM, and then he'll say 'SHOOT!'

"There's nobody that has ever hunted with Billy who has shot more ducks than him."

There was the time I almost had to shoot one of my hunting dogs. Well, he was sort of a hunting dog, a German shepherd I had named Montana who I taught to retrieve. He was my favorite dog of all-time.

Now Montana could be pretty feisty if he didn't know you, as my good friend John Stokes Sr. remembers the first time I invited him to hunt with me at Mallard Rest:

"I cannot tell why I got my first invitation to go to Mallard Rest to hunt. But every year for at least 20 years, I receive a formal invitation in the mail from Billy.

"He tells you he wants you down there at noon on a certain date. You don't get there at 12:30, you show up at 12. You don't need to be early either.

"So when I got that first-ever invitation from Billy, I thought I had really arrived. This is the best thing that ever happened to me. I've been invited to go hunting with Billy Dunavant.

"I thought maybe Billy invited me because he heard I was a good duck caller. He does not call. He gets people that can call.

"So the first time I go to Mallard Rest, it was just about dark when I got there. I got out of the car holding a gun in one hand, a duffel bag in the other hand and a duck bag.

"I started into the house. On the porch, I looked through the glass windows. There's a fire going, and there are two big German shepherds, a male and a female. I didn't think anything about it.

"So I reach out, open the door without announcing myself and take two steps in the house. The female German shepherd just growled, but the male named Montana took off. He came at me right off the ground. As he lunged, I put my hand up and he ripped it open.

"Billy said, 'We'll take you to the emergency room.' I was bleeding like a stuck hog. He wrapped a towel around it, got in the car and drove me to the emergency room in Clarksdale.

"On the way to the hospital, Billy's wife Tommie called him and said, 'You need to know something. In Mississippi, there's a law that anytime a dog seriously bites a person requiring hospital treatment they automatically kill the dog.' So Billy tells me the situation.

"Billy doesn't like the sight of blood. He stayed out in the waiting room. They deadened my hand, cleaned it, sewed it up and put a big bandage on it.

"While I was being tended to, a policeman came in with this big clipboard. He was waiting to get the name of the dog and who owned the dog. By then, I'd gotten my story figured out.

"I said, 'Officer, it was a big dog. Looked like a mongrel. He was with a pack of dogs. I have no idea who owned the dogs in the pack. But as I walked up to the house, the pack was there and this dog bit me. I have no idea where that dog is or who owns it.'

"My story saved Montana's life.

"The next day, I went hunting with the bandage. I got back to Memphis and the word got out. Scott May, who is also a hunter and an attorney, found out about it. He wrote me a letter that said, 'Stokes, you've got to be pretty dumb. If you had called me and told me about this incident, we'd own Mallard Rest. You wouldn't have to wait on the invitation.'

"I called Billy and said, 'Understand one thing. I'm not pressing charges, but you won't have to send me an invitation to come down there and hunt. I'll let you know when I'm coming.'"

As I said in "In It To Win It," I'm pretty competitive. I admit I always looked for someone to invite hunting that didn't mind competition. Ronnie Grisanti has never forgotten one of his hunting trips to Mallard Rest:

"Mr. Billy really searches for people who are very competitive because he's the most competitive person ever. We started talking hunting, and he invited me to hunt with him to see how I could shoot, to see if I was worth keeping around.

"Five or six years ago, John Stokes, Mr. Billy and myself were down at Mallard Rest. It was ideal duck hunting weather. Stokes and I were going to shoot in the morning, and Mr. Billy already had shot the night before.

"We get in the blind and Mr. Billy is calling the ducks for us. I have never seen so many ducks in my life, all these dots coming in the sky toward us. Stokes and I shoot our limit in five minutes.

"Mr. Billy says, 'You know that's a record at Mallard Rest. No one has ever shot two limits of ducks in that short a time. We go back to the house, laugh about it and John goes home.

"Later on that afternoon, we're sitting around the fire and Mr. Billy says, 'Ronnie, can you shoot tomorrow morning as well as you did this morning?' I say, 'Mr. Billy, the way the ducks are coming in, I ought to be able to.'

"Sure enough, we get up the next morning, head to the very same hole, and conditions are excellent except the ducks aren't coming in like they did the morning before.

"A lot of them still come, and Mr. Billy and I shoot our limits. He looks at me and says, 'I don't think we shot our limit as fast as y'all did yesterday, or maybe we did.' I say, 'Nah, I don't think we did, Mr. Billy. I looked at my watch and we're about five or six minutes off.' He says, 'Yeah, that's going to be hard to beat.'

"We get out of the blind and start toward the truck. About the time we get on dry land, geese fly over us. Mr. Billy throws his gun up, shoots a goose and it drops right at his feet. He reaches down, picks up the goose and says, 'Well, we won.'

"I say, 'We won what?' He says, 'We beat the record from yesterday. I say, 'Mr. Billy, what are you talking about?' He says, 'We not only shot a limit, but we shot a limit and a goose!' "

I know when some people see me shoot for the first time because of the way I hold a shotgun, they probably wonder how I'm so accurate. But like my cousin Paul Tudor Jones says, it seems to work just fine:

"You've got to realize that Billy is left-eye dominant, right handed, so he puts his head all the way over on the stock, and

shoots with his left eye looking down the barrel. It's a bit like throwing a football with your feet.

"Yet, the guy is unequivocally the greatest single wing shot I've ever seen. I've shot all over the world and I've seen them all. He's the best wing shot. Every time he'd shoot a duck, his head would perfectly fold between its wings, facedown position. I've never seen anyone consistently stone them like him."

When I went hunting in England where they only allow over-and-under guns where you load shells from the top, I filed and received a handicap permit to bring my gun that loads on the side. Of course, I never heard the end of it from my friends.

But I gave as good as I got. One time in Scotland, my friend George Barley had gotten a lease to fish on the property of the Duke of Roxbury. Because George wanted to make sure we could come back there in future years, he wanted us on our best behavior.

He was worried that I would call the Duke a "dickhead," which as you will read in my next chapter is my favorite term of endearment. So George tells Tommie his concern and she tells me.

It was information I could use to keep George in suspense. So when I would engage in conversation with the Duke, I'd pause and say "You . . ." and then I finish my sentence without saying "Dickhead." Every time I paused, George died just a little.

I have total focus when I'm hunting, so much so that one time I didn't even realize a duck blind I was sitting in on a frosty day at Mallard Rest had caught fire. The heater malfunctioned and the blind ignited. I didn't realize anything until Ronnie Grisanti, my panicked hunting companion, frantically pointed it out. I realized my pants were on fire. I threw the heater in the lake and I jumped in, also.

I have a lot of friends who hunt regularly and some who hardly hunt, like my buddy Donald Dell. He's a former U.S. Davis Cup captain and one of the best sports marketers and agents in history, but he doesn't know crap about hunting, as he readily admits:

"I don't hunt at all and the only time I did was once a year when Billy invited my wife and I to his farms in Mississippi for New Year's. Hunting scares the hell out of me because I'm not comfortable with it. It's like amateur hour when I hunt.

"Usually, we had six of us in the blind. We're drinking whiskey, and Billy's yelling and screaming every time we miss a shot. He's saying, 'Let me shoot one-handed and I bet you I can kill 10 times as many as you do.' His friends said that was a bet you didn't want to take.

"Billy had a lot of fun at my expense, Like the time Billy is so anxious to get out to the blind before daylight, he's screaming, 'You gotta get in the truck.' I said, 'I need to get a camouflage vest. Where is it?' His wife Tommie said, 'It's in the back room in a closet.'

"So I race back to the closet. I see this thing hanging in the closet. I grab it because it's camouflage and I run to the truck. I get to the blind and I try to put the thing on.

"Tommie was in the blind that day. She took one look at that damned vest I was struggling to get on and said, 'That's Bully's vest! What are YOU doing?' Of course, that was the laugh of the year, me trying to put on a vest that belonged to Billy and Tommie's dog.

"I never heard the end of it for five years. It was hysterical, and a true story unfortunately.

"Another time we were driving by a bunch of fields, Billy slams on the brakes and says, 'You gotta shoot those!' I'm not looking that close, but I see all these white things in the field. He rolls down my window and I start firing.

"It turned out to be a field full of geese decoys. That was all a set-up joke. I heard it for hours from Billy, 'How could anybody shoot the decoys?' "

One time at my ranch in Montana, I was hunting turkey when a bobcat happened upon the turkey. It worked out well. Well, sort of, as Tommie recalls:

"Billy limps in the house and he looks like he's been dragged down a road. He has scratches on his face and arms, his clothes are torn and he still has twigs and branches in his hair.

"He looks at me and says, 'Do you want the good news or the bad news? I say, 'Tell me the good news.' He says, 'I killed a turkey and a bobcat with one shot, because the bobcat was stalking the turkey.'

"When he says 'bobcat' I immediately thought he had been attacked, maybe he has rabies. Then he says, 'The bad news is I lost the car keys.' I ask, 'How did you do that?' He says, 'I was so excited about killing both the turkey and the bobcat with one shot that I fell out of the deer stand and fell through a bunch of trees. I lost the keys, so I walked back here.'

"Billy was so passionate about making the shot he didn't even realize he was hurt. He wanted us to drive back and get what he killed. I drove him to the hospital instead because he also had a concussion."

Honestly, I sometimes forget when I hunt that I have such good range. Every once in awhile, I get reminded in a duck blind by good friends such as Ducks Unlimited CEO Dale Hall:

"Billy has always focused on being very good at what he does. If he takes something on, he wants to be successful. That's definitely true in hunting.

"I've hunted with a lot of people, but I believe Billy is the best long shot I've ever seen.

"The first or second year I went hunting with him, I had turned around in the blind to get more ammunition. Billy starts yelling, 'They're in the decoys!'

"I turned around, grabbed a gun and the ducks were 50 yards out, 20 yards outside the decoys.' I said, 'Billy, just tell me as they are working in.' He said, 'You could have shot them right there.' I said, 'Okay, you shoot 'em.'

"And he dropped every of them.

"I said, 'Billy, you don't understand how good a long shot you are compared to the rest of us. All the rest of us learn to shoot at 25 to 30 yards. You think 50 yards is very reasonable.' He said, 'Yeah, that's just a good shoot.'

"Like in business, Billy always hit his target looking at the long range while everybody else was still working at that medium range."

Like my father, I passed on my love of the outdoors to my sons. It didn't take any of them long to understand that if you go hunting with me, you better have your finger on the trigger, as my oldest son Bill recalls:

"The reason all of Dad's sons shoot pretty quick is because if you don't he will. I never watch the ducks when you shoot with him. You'd never get off a shot.

"You watch his left hand. When his left hand dropped the duck call, you better have two shots off or you didn't get to shoot.

"I started hunting with Dad by myself when I was about 6 or 7 years old. He took me to Hatchie Coon and I was wearing one of those puffy polyester-hunting suits because it was freezing. Back then, there weren't any heaters in the duck blinds. They just used buckets of charcoal.

Billy founded the Mississippi Chapter of the Nature Conservancy and was presented an award by the group in 2014.

"I back up next to the charcoal bucket and catch that polyester suit on fire. The flames shot up mid-leg to my shoulders and it damned near melted on me.

"It was bad enough to where we had to get in the boat and go home. My mother was worried about how bad I was hurt. Dad was worried about screwing up the duck hunt. That's how intense he was hunting.

"That wasn't the first time I caught on fire hunting with Dad. When I was about three, he took me and my two sisters, Dot and Connie, hunting on a cold day.

"Dad brought along a little Hibachi oven to put in the duck blind so we wouldn't complain about being cold. My sisters said I was wearing rubber boots and I put my feet on the stove to keep them warm.

The first two turkeys killed at the Leatherman Plantation in Robinsonville, Mississippi.

"My boots caught on fire and started melting. My Dad started smelling the rubber as the ducks started flying past. He reaches back, grabs me with one arm and lowers me in the water to put out the fire while he's shooting at the ducks with his other arm.

"All his kids have hunted and fished all over kingdom come with him, from the salmon fishing in Quebec to the trout fishing in Alaska to the duck hunting in Mississippi and Arkansas.

"Dad will tell you there's nothing greater than to be outdoors with your children. The memories I have hunting and fishing with Dad will always be there. I try to share them with my boys, who've also gone hunting with him.

"Hunting is a great stress reliever for Dad. He's really, really good at it."

All my friends think I'm hard on them when we hunt. I can be just as tough on my family, like one of my sons, Woodson, knows all too well:

"Hunting with Dad is a fun and absolutely terrifying experience for anyone who hunts with him. The pressure to perform well when hunting with him is like no other pressure I feel in doing anything else.

"If I shoot and miss, which happens a lot, he gives you the hardest time. He knows you missed and he'll ask, 'Did you kill that duck?' Of course, my answer is 'no' because the duck is flying away.

"He's such a long shot, he can kill them stone dead at 50 yards. If the duck gets closer than 50 yards and you haven't shot it, he asks you, 'What are you waiting on?' My answer is, 'I'm waiting for him to get closer so I can make damn sure I can kill it.' That's not what he wants to hear. He's so competitive."

John, another of my sons, remembers that when we had a hunt scheduled virtually nothing would stop us:

"If I was sick the night before a hunt, Dad couldn't care less. Didn't matter if it was 10 degrees in the duck blind with a charcoal fire to keep warm and if I was throwing up. I was at the hunt and I was miserable. But it was time to shoot ducks, and he consistently got the limit.

"If you didn't get up and shoot when the duck call quit, the limit for the day would be dead in the water before you'd already shot. Dad wasn't going to say, 'It's your turn.' As he got older, he was apt to give you more shit if you missed.

"I haven't always been the best hunter, but my son Dobson is a good athlete with good hand-and-eye coordination. So now if I don't shoot well with my Dad, I just put my gun down and say, 'All right, Dobson, it's your turn, you get 'em.' "

Probably the best hunter of all my sons is Buck. I remember one time when I was calling ducks, he was looking at me and not up in the sky for any incoming ducks. I had to ask him why:

"Dad asked me, 'Son, why aren't you looking at the ducks?' I said, 'I couldn't give three shits about the ducks, because when you let go of the caller I know it's time to shoot. If I'm looking at the ducks and you drop your caller, you start shooting and I'm two seconds behind you.'

"He took great pride in his hunting and shooting. He wanted to be the best shot in the duck blind. He liked to talk shit when you missed, but I liked to talk shit back to him. He was always proud when somebody made a good shot.

"One of the rites of passage for all of Dad's sons is hearing the story about the time he went hunting with his Dad, who's my namesake.

"My Dad was in the duck blind and had to take a crap. Daddy Buck tells him to go to the other end of the blind, lean out of the back and do his business. So he does.

"A little later, the ducks fly by and they shoot the ducks. Some of the ducks are wounded, so Daddy Buck has to get in his boat, which is in the back of the blind, to go collect the ducks. The motor was propped up, so Daddy Buck had to grab the back of the motor to drop it in the water.

"But my Dad had relieved himself right on the back of the motor. Daddy Buck grabbed a pile of my Dad's crap. My Dad said he'd never been cussed out like that before in his life.

"I don't know what Daddy Buck called him, but I can only assume that is where the term 'Dickhead' originated."

There was a time where if you went hunting with me, you better have been well-rested to start the day. Randall Butler,

Billy especially loved duck hunting at his private club in Webb, Mississippi, on the Mississippi Flyway.

my brother-in-law, remembers the time a man double his age wore him out:

"Around the time that Billy married my wife's sister Tommie, he invited Tina and me down to Quail Hollow for a weekend of quail hunting.

"It was a cool Saturday morning, about 9 a.m., when we were about to set out. Right before we left, Bill Ford, who was Billy's farm manager at the time, pulls me aside and says, 'Now Mr. Randall, Mr. Billy will walk you to death out there. When you get tired, call me on the radio and I will come get you in the truck.'

"I told Billy, 'Thank you,' but I was going to try very hard to keep up. After all, I was only 30 years old and Billy was approaching 60.

"The quail hunting was fabulous. But because Quail Hollow is in Mississippi pulp wood country with rolling hills, it was also strenuous.

"Billy had two excellent setter dogs. The better dog was named Pepper. Billy made it an art to call Pepper. In that long drawn out Southern style, he'd call, 'Pehhhh Pahhh.' After two hours of walking up hills and down valleys, Pepper was worn out. She and the other dog quit hunting and fell in walking behind Billy. I was worn out too, but I thought I had made it because I outlasted the dogs.

"About that time, Bill Ford pulled up in a pickup truck. My wife and I were both relieved to see Bill, since we were exhausted and ready to head back.

"But Bill wasn't there to pick us up. Instead, he brought a fresh set of dogs to relieve the tired ones. My wife decided to ride back with Bill, but I declined Bill's offer to follow my wife's lead.

"An hour later, the hunt was finally over. My wife, in the meantime, had enough time to shower and get cleaned up before I finished hunting.

"Like my father, I passed on my love of the great outdoors to my sons."

"When I finally got back to the house, I slept all afternoon and evening. The only time I woke up was to eat dinner."

I'm happy that all my children have grown to love the outdoors like I do, like my daughter Kelli:

"The most beautiful places I've ever seen have always been with Daddy. The places he owned, the places he chose to go and the places he took us were always impeccable.

"Daddy has an appreciation for wildlife and sees beauty in the landscape like no one I have ever known. One of his great joys is riding around and just looking on the properties we're blessed to have. He looks at the birds, he looks at the land and he takes it all in with intense gratitude.

"I'm a firm believer that God is the ultimate artist and that His greatest masterpieces are the land, trees, flowers and seas. Like a fine art dealer, my Dad is a collector of God's greatest accomplishments. He marvels at the great outdoors and the beauty is never lost on him. I never knew love for the great outdoors until I saw how he loved.

"Now, as I grow older, I find myself sitting on my patio a little longer and relishing my time in the middle of nowhere more deeply."

It might seem odd that someone like me who spent his entire life making business decisions at the snap of a finger, and who lived life at such a fast pace could have the patience to sit maybe three hours in a turkey blind before seeing anything.

Well, yes, I do have a calm side. But I'm not calm inside when I'm hunting. I'm all worked up.

"Without a doubt, my favorite Dickhead — my cousin Paul Tudor Jones."

9

My Favorite Dickheads

I'M NOT QUITE SURE WHEN I STARTED SAYING IT. AND if you've never heard me say it to you, it can be rather startling.

"HEY DICKHEAD!"

It's my term of endearment. It might not be politically correct, but if I've called you Dickhead, then you're in a positive light with me.

Almost all my friends understand that. Sometimes, there's someone like my personal attorney Jim Gilliland who objects to me calling him dickhead. So I've settled on calling him "Richard Cranium." He doesn't like that much either.

I said Dickhead so frequently that my kids believed I invented the term. One time when Tommie took our daughter Kelli to see the movie *Grumpy Old Men*, Walter Matthau's character called Jack Lemmon's character "dickhead." Kelli stood up and said, "Somebody's stole Daddy's word."

I've even called my minister Rev. John Sartelle a Dickhead. It happened when we were hunting. I kept calling ducks and he kept missing shots. I'm not a patient guy and before I know it, I say, "John, you Dickhead."

Immediately, I start apologizing. I had called my minister a Dickhead. He says, "Okay, Billy, I understand there are good ones and bad ones."

We keep hunting and John keeps missing. In frustration he says, "Oh, shit!"

I look at him and say, "What did you say?" He replies, "An earthly word my brother, an earthly word."

I have Dickheads of all ages and from every walk of life, like Paul Tudor Jones.

I have no words to say how I feel about Paul. He's like a son and I am so proud of him. I've enjoyed many hunting and fishing experiences with him, many at places he has offered. He's the L.D.H. (The Little Dickhead). Paul always called me "Uncle Billy" and he always was a giver.

If Paul is the Little Dickhead, Dr. George Coors was Dr. Dickhead. George was 12 to 13 years older than me and as soon as we met there was an instant friendship. He gave me a hat that said "Chief Dickhead." He introduced me to turkey hunting. We had so many adventures and experiences they could all go in a separate book. He died in 2014 and I miss him every day.

Each of my Dickheads has made my life a little more interesting in many ways. Here are some of my favorite Dickheads who don't mind me calling them Dickhead because they know it's an earthly word:

Eli Tullis, New Orleans commodities broker: *"I met Billy when he, Frank Mitchener and I met at my house when the National Cotton Council met one year in New Orleans.*

"We all got loaded and I had a wonderful time. That was really the beginning of our relationship. He has called me 'Dickhead' longer than I can remember and I can't put in this book what I call him.

"Billy was fast, unique in his ability to know the value of cotton and how to hedge it or not hedge.

"He'd want to buy March, sell May. Then he'd want to buy May and sell July. Then he'd want to buy July and sell something else. All these orders are intertwined, but every time he sold it was ching-a-ling.

"We had our little ups and downs. He'd fire you in a heartbeat and hire you back even quicker.

"He called me up one morning and said, 'I want you to buy a deck (which are December futures).' I said, 'Okay, Billy, how many?' He said, 'I didn't say how many. I said I want you to buy a deck.'

He called me again while he's going to play tennis at 11:45. He said, 'I'm leaving. How many decks have you bought? I said, 'Billy, I bought 11,000 bales, which is 110 contracts.'

"He said, 'Dammit, I told you to buy a deck. You're fired.'

"So I bought 130 decks. He called me again and asked, 'What in the hell are you doing?' I said, 'I figured you're bullish, so I bought myself a whole lot of decks and I'm going to keep doing it.'

He said, 'What do you mean you're going to keep doing it?"

I said, 'Billy, I bought 130 decks. Do you want them?' He said, 'Yeah, dammit, I want them.'

"So I asked, 'I'm re-hired?'

"Our lifelong friendship has been a fabulous experience."

Coors Arthur, business partner of Billy's son Buck and grandson of the late Dr. George Coors: *"Granddaddy and Mr. Dunavant had a helluva lot of fun together. They knew of each other when they were younger, but they became very tight in the later portion of their lives.*

"They had a great love of duck hunting and salmon fishing. They were pranksters, both were very competitive and both were exceptional shots.

"One time they were geese hunting in Canada. Granddad put little slivers of wood behind Mr. Dunavant's trigger so he couldn't fire his gun. Mr. Dunavant got pissed off and said, 'Whoever did this ain't flying home.'

"I've seen a lot of people who can be intimidated by Mr. Dunavant in the business sense and not have the ability to have fun and make it a comfortable conversation.

Phil Burnett, former executive director of the National Cotton Council and another member of Billy's Dickhead club.

"But Granddad wasn't intimidated by Mr. Dunavant, so there was a lot of back-and-forth between them. They always had a great time together.

"A couple of duck seasons ago, John Dobbs invited me and my grandfather, Buck and his father, Neely Mallory and some other folks hunting.

"Buck and I wouldn't shoot, but we put my Granddad and Mr. Dunavant side-by-side. It was fantastic to sit back and see two guys who had seen so much in their lives just B.S. with each other, play games on each other and shoot ducks with each other.

"You don't see a friendship like that very often."

John Stokes Sr., founding partner of Morgan Keegan: *"I can't remember Billy calling me anything but Dickhead. There* *are just a handful of people in the world like him. He's one of a kind.*

"I was a young guy, younger than Billy, when I came to Memphis from Mayfield, Kentucky. A guy like me finds out who's running things, and back in the 1970s and 1980s Billy Dunavant was running things in Memphis. He was a very powerful man.

"I quickly learned Billy is an unbelievable competitor. The only other guy equal I got to know is NBA legend Jerry West, who moved to Memphis and was president of the Grizzlies for a few seasons. Billy's right in there with Jerry West in wanting to beat you. It's that important to him.

"He's one of the smartest people I've ever met. He has a fabulous mind. Back in his day Billy controlled the world cotton market, and that goes back to him being really competitive and doing what it takes to win.

"When it comes to commodities, you've got to be smart and gutsy as hell playing with millions of dollars. You've got to have a lot of faith in yourself, too. Anytime you make a trade, on the stock or cotton market, you've got to remember somebody is on the other side of that trade that thinks you're wrong.

"You can't buy something from somebody that doesn't want to sell it. I've always remembered that. If they've got better information than you do, they're going to whip you.

"Not only did Billy have guts, but he had to have a great system of information, like the ability to find out something as obscure as the weather in Siberia. He had a network of people that allowed him to know things before they happened. There's no such thing as inside information in commodities.

"Billy had to have great info. He talked to people that were on the scene. One of these days sitting there drinking with him, I'm going to say, 'Look, how was it you were always a little ahead of everybody else?' I'm going to get him to tell me.

"Success to most people means they've made a lot of money, and surely Billy has. But that isn't what makes him outstanding.

"He's got a really big heart. He's kind and generous. If he likes you or if he likes a cause, he likes you forever and that's important to me. He can put up with your weaknesses and your shadow side, because he's got a bit of it himself.

"People have no idea what he does for his friends and what he has meant to his friends.

"His favorite singer is George Strait, and he can sing along with his music.

"John Wayne is his favorite movie star. I didn't know how much Billy liked John Wayne until the time we were flying to or from Argentina on a hunting trip. Billy was watching a John Wayne movie. The movie would get sad, and I looked over at Billy and he's crying. He's into these John Wayne movies like you can't believe.

"I don't think I have a better friend today and I'd like to think Billy feels the same about me. We're that close."

Frank Mitchener, roommate at McCallie: *"After we were together in school at McCallie, I eventually went back home to North Mississippi and became a farmer.*

"Billy handled all my business. We never had a written contract for about my first 20 years with him. He told me what he was going to pay me and I said, 'Fine.' I never questioned and I never worried about it.

"Finally, his lawyers insisted he needed a written contract with me and there probably should have been one for both of our sakes, because I was raising a heck of a lot of cotton.

"If you don't know Billy, you might be taken aback by his competitiveness. But once you know Billy, you understand that's part of his personality.

"He and I share a common border of my farm and his place just east of Sumner. For years, he tried to get me to go duck hunting with him because he'd say, 'I have the finest duck hunting in the world.' That's probably true.

"I just don't enjoy duck hunting. I don't like to get up at 5 o'clock in the morning. His duck blinds are so nice you could wear your loafers out there. He'd get furious with me because I didn't enjoy it. We'd be out there, I'd raise my shotgun to shoot and he'd push me out of the way to shoot the birds.

"Yes, he was competitive but he was also a perfectionist. He has always been good to me."

Paul Tudor Jones, Billy's cousin and one of the world's leading investment advisors: *"Billy is charismatic, funny, dashing and bold.*

"He has one of the quickest wits of anybody that I've ever met. He was on point with his sincerity. When he was talking and when he was serious, you knew it, because he could get angry. He could also get very emotional and cry. He had a piercing look that drove right through your heart.

"The guy had this phenomenal capacity athletically and could modify it to do virtually anything, from shooting to tennis, to basketball. He was always No. 1. Athletically, he had the 'it' factor.

"He used to invite all the high school kids over to play H-O-R-S-E. When I was playing basketball in my teen years, he would just beat the absolute living stew out of everybody, including all the high school players. We know the guy has the most phenomenal hand-eye coordination, and you could see it in all the tennis titles he won.

"But if you played H-O-R-S-E with him, he'd make all these shots and every shot had some little trick to it. It would also have a catchphrase to go with it. He'd say, 'Okay, I'm going to make this shot with my eyes closed, and it's going to come right out your ass.'

"Billy invented trash talking before they even started it in the NBA. His trash talking would make an NBA player blush."

"John Stokes, a very, very dear friend and hunting companion and a true Dickhead."

John Calipari, current Kentucky and former University of Memphis basketball coach: *"Paul Tudor Jones was trying to get me to take the Memphis job in March 2000. He was flying somewhere on a plane and we talked for 45 minutes.*

"He said, 'If you take the job, I will introduce you to five people in that city. Those people will be able to help you. They've got airplanes, they can buy tickets, they can do all the things you need to have done.' The first person on the list was Paul's 'Uncle Billy.'

"Since then, Billy and I have been great friends. One of the many things I loved about him is I could vent with him. I could go crazy and he'd just sit there and listen. He'd say, 'Okay, are you done? Are you finished? Let me deal with it. Just relax. It will be fine.'

"In all the times there when I needed help, like 'I need you to buy 2,000 tickets upstairs' or 'I need you to fly me somewhere' or

'I need some cash for locker room improvements,' he never said, 'No.'

"Billy has a kind heart. He's about people and he's so unpretentious. You'd never know he had wealth, and it wasn't what our relationship was about.

"Billy made a lot of money for a lot of people, not just for himself. He took care of a lot of people, and not just the business he was in. That, for me, means more than he was a genius in his field.

"People that move me have a heart for others, they make sure they never forget anybody along the way. That's who Billy Dunavant is.

"He's compassionate and serving. I've told his wife Tommie, 'When you consider the lives he has touched, the lives he has changed, the causes he has been a part of, Billy's led a good life.'

"He has a great sense of humor. One week, he wanted me to have lunch with him and we're in the middle of our summer camp. He was dressed in slacks and a shirt, and I walked in wearing shorts.

"He looked at me and said, 'What the hell are you doing?' I said, 'I'm in the middle of camp, you invite me to lunch, so I'm in shorts.'

"So the next time I came to see him, he had shorts on. He had the skinniest legs I've ever seen in my life.

"He's a competitive sucker, whether he's hunting, playing tennis or in business. The reason Billy was so good in business is he approached it from the standpoint of a world-class athlete. World-class athletes are always self-critical, always looking for ways to improve, even the smallest piece. Sometimes, a bunch of those small pieces puts you to another level and you say, 'How did this all happen?'

"Billy's sport was his business and the money that came with it was the winning and losing.

"We still talk at least once a week. I can say this about Billy and his life. Who's had more fun than him? Not many."

John Dobbs Sr., owner of Memphis-based Dobbs Management Services: *"Billy had more self-confidence than anybody I've ever known. He always thought he was a better athlete. He thought he was a better businessman. He was right. He was a better businessman.*

"I was always worried if I had some money this year if I was going to have it next year. Billy always had confidence that he could make a lot of money this year and then make a lot of money again the next year.

"He's not perfect. He's very hard-headed. I don't care if it's his wife, his girlfriend, his pilot, the people working for him, his children – it's either his way or the highway. That's the mark of a strong guy.

"Women absolutely loved him. Maybe because of his flamboyant personality, his high-flying style. Whatever it was, he never went anyplace where some woman didn't start hanging on to his coattails and wasn't crazy about him.

"It wasn't his fault. It just happened. He was a very faithful guy though I like to kid him about it. When we were honoring Billy on his 80th birthday, I got up to the podium and said, 'I have this telegram from Cuba. It says, 'Dear Mr. Dunavant, Gerarmo is now 19 years old. He's wondering where you are.'

"The whole time we were young, Billy did a lot of leading, taking his friends to do things they couldn't do. He'd have a farm for a dove hunt, and nobody else had a farm. He had an airplane and he'd take you to watch the University of Memphis in NCAA regional playoffs in Kansas City. He had things nobody else had, but he'd take his friends along with him.

"He was very generous. He took friends hunting and fishing all over the world, from Cuba to Spain to England. Money was something he didn't worry about. If it cost him $50,000, it cost him $50,000.

"Billy has been a great friend, and he's done lot for me. I'm sure if I came to him and said, 'Billy, I've got a problem. I need $10 million,' he'd give it to me.'

"He has been a great citizen of Memphis. He has done more good than anybody I've ever met."

John Dobbs Jr.: *"As a little kid, I chose my own godfather. I picked the guy who was the most engaging, charismatic guy I knew. That was Billy Dunavant. I felt special around him. He said I'm his only godchild. He wasn't letting anyone else be his godchild.*

"He has that magnetic personality that everybody enjoys being around. You always want to be around Billy. He'll call every once in awhile to give me a hard time about something, enough to know he's still connected.

"I once went to lunch with him to learn some of his business secrets and get an understanding. He couldn't tell me anything he'd done. He had that ability to deflect his success.

"Billy got me to give the largest donation I've ever given to anybody. He called me up, asked for it and I said 'yes' on the spot. I didn't even think about it. Because he's always done things to help me, I try to figure ways to return the favors.

"I've told my father Billy is one of my heroes."

Henry Morgan, co-chairman of Boyle Investment Company: *"Billy is like all of us. He's not perfect, but he's one of the most loyal and generous people I've ever known.*

"He is a brilliant businessman, but he has never flaunted his success or his wealth.

"We didn't grow up together, but we eventually started playing tennis together and he always beat me.

"He asked me to go hunting in Alberta, Canada, and we started going every year for 15 years spending a week to 10 days hunting

together. It was just a grand time hunting out in the middle of nowhere in a tiny town named Consort.

"There, our local confidant and goose hunting expert was Bob Day, who owned this little motel where we stayed. He was a recovering alcoholic and a good Irishman. He was so much fun to be with and a great source of information.

"The one thing you noticed about Billy was his photographic memory. For years, the only telephone available was in the motel office, yet Billy would get on this phone using no notes on his positions when he was trading cotton.

"A lot of times, we'd be driving around scouting for hunting spots, so we'd play Trivial Pursuit as we drove. He could remember historical events but he didn't know trivia like music, such as the names of bands or songs. He's so competitive he would be furious when I beat him on that junk. I seldom beat him on anything.

"We'd scout fields trying to figure out exactly the feeding spot for geese. You'd have to figure out how to get to that spot the next morning in the dark.

"One morning, we were driving trying to find the spot we found the night before in this field that had a lake. Billy was furious because we couldn't find the spot.

"Finally, we stopped. I hopped out of the truck to take a look. He said, 'Where's the lake?' I said, 'Billy, we're in the lake.' He had driven into the shallow part of the lake, which made him mad as hell.

"Another year on a Canadian trip, we shot a bunch of geese and we breasted them, which is illegal.

"The authorities found some of the carcasses, and we knew they were after us. So we gave the breasted geese away and got some geese that were legitimately cleaned.

"We were all loaded on Billy's plane ready to head home when we saw all these flashing lights. It was the Canadian Royal Mounties. They thought they were going to catch us with the illegally breasted geese, which we did not have.

"I'm flattered to be one of Billy's dickheads. It's an honor."

Coleman Connell, McVean Trading and Investments: *"Mr. D and my dad Oscar Connell were very good friends. We have a cotton farm in Clarksdale, Mississippi, and Mr. D bought my dad's cotton every year. I've been a commodities broker at McVean Trading for 25 years, and my fascination with commodities started by listening to Mr. D and my dad talk business.*

"I was always very impressed with the amount of money Mr. D made trading cotton. But he had his hands in a lot of fires – the cotton business, The Racquet Club, the Showboats, all his hunting and fishing.

"He was like that his entire career. Extremely driven, with a very sharp quick mind, an unbridled amount of energy and passion for his work. He went at his own pace, which was wide open.

"The successful people in the commodities business are the ones with the guts and money. One without the other won't do.

Very successful commodities traders like Billy Dunavant, and the guys I work for, Charlie McVean and Mike Wharton, have guts and money.

"Mr. D has friends of all ages, like I'm almost 30 years younger than him. I think the wide age range of his friends has kept him young a long time. He has so much more energy than people his age and for the longest time he had more energy of people younger than him.

"I've always just tried to be the best farmer in my side of the county and I can't even do that. But here's Mr. D, like a couple of other of my friends, who absolutely were the best in the world in their professions.

"That blows my mind. I'm fortunate to have somebody as influential in my life as Mr. D."

Neely Mallory, chairman of Mallory Alexander International Logistics: *"We've been friends since we were teenagers.*

We began going hunting and fishing together, then played golf and tennis together. Our kids have hunted together. We've just been simpatico from the very beginning. We just blended well all these years, maybe because he's a man of his word in anything he does.

"We had a partnership in a cotton warehouse for many, many years. I'd been handling Billy's cotton as a merchant until I was down in New Orleans for the LSU-Ole Miss football game played over in Baton Rouge.

"I walked into Brennan's for brunch and he was walking out. I'd had a big night of partying and he said, 'Neely, you don't look like you feel very good.' I said, 'I don't.' He said, 'I'm going to make you feel worse. I've bought a cotton warehouse in Memphis and I'm not going to send you any more cotton.'

I said, 'Dunavant, I thought you were really smart. But you're a really dumb bastard if you don't let me run it for you.' He said, 'Call me Monday.'

"I called him Monday and the result of that one conversation is we had at one time 4 million to 5 million square feet of cotton operations all across the United States. I guess calling him a 'dumb bastard' got his attention.

"But he wasn't dumb. He was a great leader, a smart guy. Whether you were bankers dealing with the finances, farmers dealing with the cotton or people running the warehouse, Billy had complete faith the job would be done correctly.

"He was just an inspirational leader, there was nothing pompous about him. All the people that worked for Billy admired him. They did what he told them to do, and when you put all the parts together Dunavant Enterprises was a gold mine that revolutionized the cotton business.

"Billy has always been a fun guy to be around. He can give you a lot of mouth and take a lot of mouth, too.

"One time when he owned the USFL pro football team, the Showboats, I mentioned how I kicked a game-winning field goal

when I was in high school. So he says, 'I'll give you 50 kicks from 30 yards out at halftime of a Showboats game, and bet you $100 a kick. I'll give you $100 when you make a kick, you give me $100 when you miss.'

"So I took the bet. I trained for weeks. Every morning when I'd drive to work, I'd stop at a high school field and kick field goals. I was ready to win the bet.

"But when the game approaches in which I'm supposed to kick at the half, Billy tells me the bet is off. 'Not enough time to do it, because the band is on the field for most of the half,' he said.

"He was very competitive. Because he hated to lose, you never forgot the times you beat him in anything he challenged you in.

"One time, he took four couples salmon fishing in Iceland. On the plane, the boys sat together. We played gin rummy all the way to Iceland and all the back from Iceland, going through London. And Billy never won a game. (George) Coors and I beat Billy and T.C. Buford to death.

"It was great. He always beat me in tennis, but I got his ass in gin.

"Our friendship is hard to put into words. When he asked you to do something, you just did it. And vice-versa."

Chuck Smith, president of National Guard Products: *"We started playing tennis against each other in tournaments at The Racquet Club. Then he invited me to play with him at the club at noon during the week.*

"We'd usually play from 12 to about 1:15 to 1:30 outside during the hottest time of the year. When we finished, I'd get to the locker room and collapse in a pool of sweat. Billy, who's 16 years older than me, was just sprinting around the locker room eating one-half of a club sandwich and drinking a Diet Mountain Dew which was waiting on him every day when we finished.

"Because he owned The Racquet Club, he had a private shower built next to his locker so he could take a shower and eat his club

sandwich at the same time. I don't know how the bread didn't get soggy.

"This was before the days of cell phones, so he had a telephone installed adjacent to his locker. Every day at the same time, he'd get a call on what the cotton market was doing. He'd give instructions on what to do.

"By now, he's finished eating his sandwich, he's got his necktie half on while he's getting dressed still talking on the phone. He hangs up the phone, finishes tying his tie and says, 'Can you play next Tuesday?' as he runs out the door.

"I'm still on the floor in a pool of sweat and I'm so tired I can't even speak.

"We did that many times over the years. I said to myself while it was happening, 'I'm really going to miss when we can no longer do this.' And I do miss it.

"It was great to be with Billy during that time period, to witness his aggressiveness and his focus. When we got out on that tennis court, it didn't matter what the cotton market was doing. For an hour and 15 minutes, all he wanted to do was kick my butt and I felt the same way.

"If we played 10 sets, he'd win eight. It may not have been a rivalry for Billy but it was for me. He would grind as hard as I did, and it taught me much about being tenacious, focused and how to set a goal and work towards it.

"Just on that little 'ol tennis court outside in the summer, there were some tremendous lessons learned.

"We finally stopped playing tennis, but got re-acquainted through duck hunting. I was a volunteer for Ducks Unlimited and Billy was singularly responsible for Ducks Unlimited moving their headquarters from Chicago to Memphis.

"We've also duck hunted at each other's farm, like a home-and-home series for 20 years.

"I've also done several international trips with him, like salmon fishing in Iceland and hunting in England at Lady Biddick's castle.

"That was an incredible trip. Lady Biddick was a piece of work. We think she had a crush on Billy, so we all played that to the hilt.

"One night I walked past her room and she called me in. She's in bed looking at this atlas opened up to the state of Mississippi. She's looking for the town of Coffeeville, because she said Billy invited her to his farm in Coffeeville. I said, 'When did Billy invite you to come?' She said, 'He didn't say.'

"It's very special to have one-on-one time with Billy, because he's focused only on you, asking questions about you, your life and your kids. There are a lot of guys who like to talk about themselves, but Billy was never like that."

Donald Dell, former Davis Cup captain and founder of ProServ, one of the first sports marketing firms in the U.S.: *"Whenever I would come down to Memphis, we'd play tennis and I'd stay at his house. Then Billy started inviting my wife and me down to his farm in the Mississippi Delta to spend New Year's with him and one or two other couples. We'd go duck hunting.*

"Billy went to Wimbledon with me. He went to the French Open. He went to the U.S. Open, though he didn't like New York much at the time. Our families became great friends.

"Billy would bet on anything. On one of those New Year's hunting trips to Mississippi, one of the guests said, 'Let's have a bet. Let's have Donald play tennis against Billy wearing waders.'

"We go out on this court and play a set with me wearing these damned waders. I beat him and it just killed him. I rode him about that for maybe five years.

"When you cut through all the kidding and the needling, what's underneath all that is someone who's madly in love with

Tommie and who really cares about his friends. He has a generous, caring heart.

"He's got a lot of good, casual friends, but he's got more lifelong friends all over the world. That's because of the way he has conducted himself.

"There's not a more loyal friend than Billy. I always had the feeling that if I ever got into trouble and needed $1 million, all I would have to do is call Billy and he'd probably bail me out. He's just that kind of friend.

"I never claimed to know anything about the cotton business. What always fascinated me about Billy and the cotton business was he could make a trade anywhere – driving in a car, in a duck blind – and he kept everything he needed to know about a deal in his head.

"I said, 'Billy, how do you remember all this?' He said, 'I keep it my head, you dumb shit. I can remember stuff.' I'm thinking, 'Jesus, somebody is going to get screwed if he forgets anything.'

"Billy has one of the most amazing personalities. He had a tremendous line of credit because he was such a well-respected businessman on a verbal handshake basis. He had leverage in the business because all the banks wanted to do business with him.

"His brainpower, his intellect, his personality and the way he carried himself got him tremendous lines of credit. No bank ever worried about not being paid back.

"I always believed Billy could run for mayor of Memphis and win hands down. He never wanted to run. I'd always push him and say, 'Why don't you run for Congress? Why don't you run for Mayor?' He'd say, 'Why would I want to do that for, for Christ sake?' I'd say, 'It would give you something else to do besides making millions off that stupid-ass cotton you're selling.'

"I think my relationship with Billy over time was more genuine and lasting. I never worked for Billy and I never owed him anything. My job didn't depend on if I offended him or if he of-

fended me, so I didn't have to be careful around him. We could tease each other very hard and we both liked that."

Rev. John Sartelle, Billy and Tommie's minister: *"When I moved to Memphis in 1977 as the minister at Independent Presbyterian, Billy's grandmother attended that church. I never met her and she died within my first month on the job.*

"Billy called me to inform me she had died. I met Billy and from that meeting there was an immediate friendship.

"I came to Memphis into a difficult situation, but Billy embraced me as a long-time Memphian. It was him saying to everyone, 'This guy is with me.' He didn't have to do that. He made me feel immediately welcome in Memphis. He became a member of Independent.

"In the South, there is a value built on loyalty. The definition of friendship for Billy is loyalty, just as in business where a good businessman to Billy is someone who's trustworthy and whose word is his bond.

"Billy and I look at friendship the same way. You can't be friends with someone without trust and loyalty.

"With Billy, what you see is what you get. There is no pretense there.

"I've always admired people of position and wealth who would be the same if they didn't have that position and that wealth. Having those things can change people, but it didn't with Billy.

"He treats everybody with respect and dignity, from people with his position and similar wealth, to the farmhands on his properties who may not have the same education.

"Billy is an individual who cares about people. When he meets them, he talks to them, asks them questions. It doesn't matter about their background, who they are, where they come from or how wealthy they are. He doesn't look down his nose ever.

"He worked hard to get where he is, it did not come easy. He's extremely smart. God gifted him with astute business acumen.

He was very diligent and very ethical. He'd stick by his word, even if it cost him a lot of money. He wanted to keep his word.

"Billy cares about his relationship with the Lord. When I first met Billy, we'd talk about it. He's always had a serious faith and it caused him to be circumspective about his wealth.

"He has always understood where it came from. He understood the Lord blessed him, that he's not a self-made man. There's a difference between 'I am brilliant in business, look what I've done' and 'God gave me the gift of business acumen.'

"Billy and I have talked about the temptation of the powerful and the wealthy is to think you're self-made people. Most people I know who have that power and that wealth have that self-made arrogance about them.

"There's a book called Turtle on a Fencepost. *If you're from the country like I am, you know that someone put that turtle on top of the post. Billy spiritually understands how he got on top of the post.*

"If the Lord says to Billy, 'Billy, why should I welcome you to my kingdom?', Billy is not going to say, 'Because I'm good.' He's going to say, 'Because Christ has died.' He really understands that. He understands he's a sinner who needs a Savior. Not everyone can understand it, but that's exactly where Billy is."

Jim Gilliland, Billy's personal attorney: *"I've been his friend as long as I remember. He's said that I've been through more major crises with him than his wives.*

"We grew up on different sides of Walnut Grove Road, but all the neighborhood boys like Billy would play football on a vacant lot next to my house on Galloway. One of the neighbors' dads put in a basketball goal.

"Billy was a skeet shooter. None of us knew what shooting skeet was about, but we were impressed when he got his name in the paper when he won skeet shooting competitions.

"He's nine months older than me, a grade ahead of me in school. We went off to high school in different places, and then I got to Vanderbilt just as he was leaving to go home to Memphis to work for his father and attend the University of Memphis.

"It was sometime in the 1970s when things got a bit complicated in the cotton business and Billy said he needed my legal help. That's how we started our business relationship.

"It helped that I wasn't a Dunavant Enterprises employee. I was his attorney. So when he got fussy about something when he disagreed with me, there wasn't much he could do. It never occurred to me he might want to get another lawyer.

"I was Billy's first line of defense in almost any venture he considered. He was a quick study, who'd see the big picture and assess the direction he should be going.

"Then when I got into it, I was the guy who was looking for all the traps and downside. We'd go over things and I'd say, 'Nah, hell nah, I'm not about to get us in that.' Then he'd come back and say he wanted to take the risk. Then I'd say, 'Billy, you need to understand what you're doing. This thing will bite you in the ass.'

"Don't assume Billy always had a magic touch. Not everything he invested in worked. Investing in water slides was the worst of all. I complained about that one. Billy put the money into the business, and then had to tear down the slide. He lost all the investment costs and after all of that he still had to pay rent on the land where the slide had been. Luckily, it wasn't a big enough deal to make a financial impact.

"My wife Lucia and I have known Billy and all three of his wives. He and Tommie are a good match. Lucia and I got involved with that relationship early on when Billy called me one night about 8 o'clock.

"Now, to get a call from Billy at 8 o'clock is unusual. He usually has on his nightcap and nightgown to go to sleep about the time the sun sets. So it was surprising when I got that call and he says

in a nice, sweet voice I'm unaccustomed to hearing, 'Hey, I've been thinking about going to Australia. Would you and Lucia like to fly down with me?'

"Then, about two minutes into the conversation he tells me he's got somebody going with him.

"He had two gins down in the Australian Outback that he just opened. I told him, 'Sure, it would be nice to go.'

"I figured out later that Billy had invited Tommie to go to Australia with him on his plane and Tommie asked, 'Who else is going?' Billy said, 'Business associates.' She said, 'No.' Then apparently, the solution was to make Lucia and me the chaperones so it would be presentable for them to travel together.

"We had a wonderful time in Australia. But it was perfectly clear Billy had very little interest in spending a week with Lucia and me as much as he did spending a week with Tommie.

"You have a limited number of old friends in life. Billy has been a true friend for a long time. I just love the guy."

Phil Burnett, former CEO of the National Cotton Council: *"Billy has been an energetic, focused, highly intelligent and extremely competitive guy from the first day we met. You can see and feel his energy.*

"What made him successful was his ability to see the need for change and try to make that change, and his willingness to accept risk and manage that risk. In the business he was in, that was paramount to being successful.

"He had a wonderful organization with extremely capable employees, but he was on top of everything. He really knew what was going in within that business.

"You could be duck hunting or traveling with him, and he'd get on the phone working his inventory, making multimillion-dollar deals and not even looking at a note. He'd just pull infomation out of his head and make a deal without hesitation.

"I've seen him in planes, limos, cars, duck blinds, fishing boats making multimillion-dollar deals. I've been in business a long time, so when I make a tough decision, I like to get in a comfortable environment where I'm not distracted and I can think about it. Billy could take a call anywhere at anytime to do those things. That set him apart.

"He's smart, honest and a man of integrity. He loved the cotton industry and still does. He might moan, 'I'm glad I don't have to do that anymore,' but he misses it.

"I've hunted in Mississippi with him and I've fished with him in Montana. He's a lot of fun to fish with. I'm not much of a fisherman, so what I've learned I've learned from him. He always has a competitive nature.

"One day we were fishing on this beautiful little river and he asked me how many fish I caught. I probably snagged my line in the trees as many times as I hooked a fish, but I gave him a number. He knew the exact number of fish I pulled in, how many I'd lost and how many trees I'd been in.

"When we were hunting, he'd always try to make sure the experience was enjoyable for us. He worried about that. He worried about the guy coming the next day. Was he going to have a good experience? You want him to enjoy what he's doing in the moment, but he's always one step ahead of you.

"One of the things that has impressed me about Billy over the years was his philanthropy and his generosity trying to do good for Memphis, this region and this country. When Billy sees something he believes in, he makes it work.

"He's a true and loyal friend, and he has been a big part of my personal and business life. He was there for me and stood by me when I went through a tough personal time going through a divorce.

"He's also fussed at me, but that's one of the things that makes him different. He says a lot of things that a lot of people think, but won't say. He doesn't hold back when it's time to let it go. Some-

times, he's a little hard on folks, but he comes back and everything is okay.

"That's good and bad, but it's worked for him over the years. He's quick to criticize when he thinks you need it, but he also gives you praise.

"Billy's close friends will walk on fire for him."

Ronnie Grisanti, Memphis restaurateur: *"I've known Billy almost 25 years from the moment he started coming in the restaurant, and I cooked for him. I can't name all the things he's done for me.*

"He never pulls any punches and he tells you exactly like it is. He doesn't sugarcoat anything. What's wrong is wrong, what's right is right."

Trow Gillespie, who has worked with Billy on many charitable causes: *"One day, I got an invitation to Billy's Christmas party. And I said, 'I have finally arrived in Memphis, this is a really big deal.' He had two shifts to his party and I was invited with the other turkeys in the first shift. My wife went out and bought a new dress. I was right on time. I said to myself, 'This is a great evening.'*

"I walked in and said, 'Hey Billy.' He said, 'Hey Dickhead.' I thought, 'I've already pissed him off and I hadn't had a drink yet.' Then I learned four years later that was a very big compliment."

Woods Eastland, former board member of the New York Cotton Exchange: *"I got to know Billy when we were both on the board of the New York Cotton Exchange in the early 1990s. The board would meet six times a year. In the beginning, I'd fly commercial to and from New York. But Billy eventually asked me to fly on his plane with him. I really got to know him well during those two-hour plane rides and we hit it off really well. We ate dinner together several times.*

"We also had a business relationship. Our company sold Billy's company a lot of cotton.

"He's a very unusual person because he combines brains, judgment and courage.

"If we all could go back in time 30 years and we could have one wish, a lot of us would like to make several hundred million dollars. Most of us don't want to make the sacrifice to do that. But Billy's extremely driven.

"First of all for a guy to amass the wealth he has amassed, he meets every man on the same terms. Billy really never has outgrown the fact he's a Memphis kid that came from a family with great values.

"He's just fun to be with. I've never had a time where I've been with him that I didn't enjoy it."

When I think of what all my Dickheads have meant to me, how they shared their laughs and lives with me, my favorite singer George Strait sings it best in his song "Living and Living Well," when he says:

"There's a difference in living and living well,
You can't have it all by yourself,
Something's always missing
'Til you share it with someone else
There's a difference in living and living well."

I love all my Dickheads. Even Richard Cranium.

In 1984, Billy was presented the highest award from the National Conference of Christians and Jews. Howard Cosell was the keynote speaker.

10

Wild Hairs

I'VE BEEN A LITTLE BOY ALL MY LIFE. I HAVE MY serious moments, but I like to jack around and play. I lived to play, but I'd work it into my business.

If you know me, I'm a spur of the moment guy. So if I wanted to go hunting with friends in Cuba, I did it. If I wanted to schedule one afternoon to hop on my plane to kill a deer at my Texas ranch that happened to appear about the same time every day, I did it. And if I wanted to run for President of the United States . . .

Well, I actually thought about it for 18 months before I realized I was full of crap and that I couldn't see myself handling an international crisis if turkey season happened along at the same time.

I think Jimmy Carter was the president at that time, but he wasn't a very good one. I guarantee you I could have done as well as he did.

I wasn't even going to start out running for Congress and eventually run for president. I was going to straight up run for president, and it didn't matter that I had no political experience or any platform.

At that point and time in my career, I thought I was good enough to do it. I bounced the idea off some of my friends. I don't think anybody ever encouraged me to do it. Some of them probably said, "Billy, that's an interesting idea."

My closest friends, like my buddy John Dobbs Sr., didn't mince words when I called him:

"Billy calls me and tells me, 'I'm thinking about running for president.' I say, 'President of what?' He says, 'President of the United States.' I told him, 'You crazy son-of-a-bitch. If you think you can run for president, a monkey is going to jump out of my ass. Billy, I know you're good, but you ain't that good.' "

I'm glad I didn't do that. That would have cost me a lot of money in campaign contributions.

Later on, when I really thought about it, maybe some of the baggage I was carrying from previous marriages wouldn't go well running for president. I think my outdoor life also overruled it. I love to hunt and fish in season, and the thought of not being able to do that where and when I wanted dampened my White House aspirations.

Also, some of my long-time Dunavant employees and confidants, like Louis Baioni, who was my treasurer, said I just wasn't a fit in politics:

"Running for president wouldn't have worked for Billy. He's too honest. He couldn't tell lies with a straight face."

My life moved at such a good pace that I probably jumped past my running-for-president phase pretty quick. If you know me, I had to keep moving. I always loved the next adventure, like the time I decided to go quail and duck hunting in Cuba with John Dobbs and Clarence Bowe, who ran my Arizona office for years.

It was probably in the late 1950s, just before Cuban dictator Fulgencio Batista was overthrown by Fidel Castro. My daddy used to go down to Cuba all the time, because it has great fishing and hunting.

Cuba is only about an hour from New Orleans by plane. I had a letter from the Batista government permitting us entry into the country to hunt, so we all flew down there.

One night, we were driving down a dark road when we were stopped by eight, maybe ten armed guards at a roadblock. I guess we didn't look like lost tourists since we were all wearing khaki clothes.

They got us out of the car and circled us. When they looked in our trunk and saw all our guns and ammunition, they must have thought we were getting ready to take over Cuba. They clicked off the safeties on their guns. I thought John Dobbs was going to faint. He remembers like it happened last week:

"My Dad was very nervous about me going down there with Billy, because Batista was about to be overthrown. But Billy didn't think anything of it. We had a guide named Jose and a letter from the Batista government. We go in, hunt, get out, no problem, according to Billy.

"But when we got stopped, those guards surrounded us with pointed guns after finding 10 shotguns and five cases of shells in the trunk. I was scared to death. The guards put me in a car by myself, and Billy and Clarence went off together with guards in a separate car.

"They took us to police headquarters. Once they saw we had a letter from the Batista government, they cleared us. If they hadn't, we'd all probably still be rotting in a Cuban prison."

I don't think I ever went back to Cuba. I had too many other hunting and fishing options, especially on the properties I own in Montana, Mississippi and Texas.

Sometimes, my trips didn't get off to ideal starts, like the time my pilot Joe Castleman and I landed in Prescott, Maine, where I often fished. Joe remembers our timing was great that day:

"It so happened that day they were having a dedication at the airport because they had re-modeled the terminal.

Bob Hope greets Billy at the American Cotton Shippers Association meeting, when Billy was president of the Association.

"The airport was so small there wasn't even much ground to park planes. So when I dropped Billy and turned around the jet to leave, the jet exhaust blew all the windows out of the terminal during the dedication ceremony. Of course, we paid for it all."

I'm standing there with all my fishing gear when Joe spun the plane to leave. The dedication ceremony ended quickly when all the windows got blown out. I wasn't embarrassed. They built a shitty airport with shitty windows. I didn't volunteer to pay to replace the windows, but they hinted that I should.

There was this time that David Belew, who manages my property in Vernon, Texas, called to tell me of a sure kill that began to appear every afternoon like clockwork. When David told me about this deer that showed up every day at 4:30 in the same place, I put it on my schedule. Tommie and I flew out of Memphis at about 3 one afternoon wearing camo.

We went straight to the deer stand. At 4:45, there's no deer. Five minutes later, no deer. Ten minutes later at 5 o'clock, no deer. So I pick up the phone, call David and say, "It's 5 o' clock. Where is that damned deer?" We gave the deer a little more time. Finally at 5:30, he came and I shot him twice. We didn't find him until the next morning, but it was a real trophy. We have him hanging in our farm in Coffeeville.

It was at my Coffeeville property that I once kept two lions and a bear. I'm sure my friends thought I was crazy, but I'd go down to Mississippi every weekend and play with those lions.

Like a dumbass, I'd get in the cage with them. I'd knock 'em in the head, playfully beat on 'em a bit and they'd knock me down with a swat of their paw. They never really hurt me, and I didn't think they were going to eat me.

I had a bear, but one winter after he didn't move for a couple of days, I thought he was dead. I had a doctor pronounce him dead, so I buried him.

Bears tend to hibernate in caves. But because it was winter, the story got around that I buried a bear that was actually hibernating and not dead. I caught so much crap for it. John Dobbs recalls a condescending letter I received from a doctor:

"After Billy buries the bear, some doctor reads about it in a magazine. He writes Billy a letter telling him how stupid he is for killing the bear, because the doctor thought the bear was alive but hibernating. Billy writes him a letter back. It says, 'Dear Dr. Jones, I know whether a bear is hibernating or a bear is dead. I'm telling you this bear was dead. The M.D. after your name must mean Mule Dick.' "

I love to mess with people, especially those closest to me. Sometimes, I do stuff just to see if I can get a reaction. Tommie remembers a couple of times where she thought I went over the edge:

"Billy and I hadn't been married very long when we had my Mom and Dad over for dinner at our house in Memphis. We were sitting there with our daughter Kelli.

"We all started talking about how hard it was for women to find bathing suits when you don't like trying them on in dressing rooms. Billy says, 'I don't have any problems with bathing suits.' So he just leaves the room.

"The next thing I know, he comes back in the room wearing Kelli's black-and-white striped Calvin Klein bathing suit and a coverup like he's going to the beach. He stuffed towels in the cleavage area. Thank God it was a one-piece suit. I don't even know what possessed Billy to do that. He wasn't drunk.

"Then another time at our ranch in Montana, Dan Groshens, who's our ranch conservationist and Billy's hunting and fishing guide, walks in our house one morning during one of the times my mother was visiting us.

"Billy greets Dan wearing a big-brimmed fishing hat, some laced-up fishing boots, fishing shorts and my mother's nightgown. At that point, Dan hadn't been working for us long. He looked at Billy, didn't say a word and turned around and walked out. He must have thought he was a crossdresser."

Tommie is so trusting and loving I can tell her almost anything with a straight face and she believes it. I can string her along pretty good, but every once in awhile she calls my bluff.

Evidence of that is a trumpet in a glass case hanging on a wall in the third floor loft of our Montana ranch house. When people see the trumpet with a Persian proverb inscription, they must wonder, "Why in the hell is this trumpet hanging here?" I'm going to let Tommie tell you, as Paul Harvey used to say, the rest of the story:

"I'm someone who really can sing. In my previous life before Billy, I'd sing at church. I'd sing at events and play the piano.

"Every time our daughter Kelli would say, 'My mom can sing and play the piano,' Billy would say, 'You haven't heard me play the trumpet.' I'd say, 'Billy, you can't play the trumpet.' He'd say, 'Of course I can play the trumpet. Certainly I can play the trumpet. I can't believe you don't think I'm telling the truth.'

"Every time Billy's ability to play the trumpet was mentioned, his story would get longer and more lavish. He'd claim he played the trumpet in high school. He played a certain type of trumpet and he loved to play for his mother.

"When Billy and I were about to celebrate our second wedding anniversary, I tell Kelli one day, 'Mom doesn't know what to get Dad. He's got so much, he'll want something special.'

"She says, 'Oh Mom, get Daddy a trumpet. We need to research and find the exact trumpet he would have played in high school. I can't believe what his face will be like when you give it to him.'

"So we did exactly that. Of course, the trumpet Billy supposedly played in high school was antique. It was not cheap and I paid for it with my own money. We get this trumpet, take it to a music store and they show us the exact mouthpiece needed.

"I decide I'm going to give Billy his trumpet while we're on his plane going to one of our previous vacation homes in Maine. Before we leave, Kelli tells me, 'You've just got to take a picture of Daddy's face when he sees the trumpet.'

"I'm so excited to give him his trumpet. I'm thinking, 'This is the best anniversary present ever.' I give Billy the wrapped trumpet. He opens it and you should have seen the shocked look on his face.

"I'm thinking, 'Oh my God, you're so excited, I've gotten the best present for you.' I tell him, 'Try it out.'

"He puts the mouthpiece on, raises the trumpet to his lips and says, 'It's the wrong mouthpiece.' I say, 'It's not the wrong mouthpiece. The guy at the music store showed me how to do it.'

"Finally he admits to me he can't play. I say, 'You're telling Kelli, not me.'

"So Billy decides he can't tell Kelli the truth because she's just a little girl and he'll hurt her feelings. He gets the idea that he'll have one of his friends who plays the trumpet, Louis Baioni, to teach him to play one song.

"But Billy couldn't even do that. He can't even learn to play one song; he can't even blow through the mouthpiece. Finally, he has to tell Kelli.

"I took the trumpet and said, 'Eventually this trumpet is going to show up again'. I framed it, put it up there in the African room loft with a Persian proverb that reads, 'Don't let your tongue cut off your head.'

"Basically, it means don't let your mouth overload your ass. Billy used our trumpet story when he gave a talk at a stockholders meeting to illustrate about not getting so deep in it you can't back it up."

Family members usually were the targets of my playfulness. My sweet niece Rachel Butler has never forgotten one of her trips to my house:

"When I was in kindergarten, my family and I made a trip to Memphis to see Uncle Billy and Aunt Tommie. On this particular day, I wore a blue outfit with green apples on it and a brand new pair of sandals that I was very proud of.

"Uncle Billy always likes playing jokes on me. So when I got out of the car that day, he snatched off one of my sandals and threw it in a tree! Everybody had a pretty good laugh about it, but when Uncle Billy tried to get my shoe back down it was stuck.

"He shook the tree and shook the tree and shook the tree, but the shoe wasn't budging. Finally, he got Mr. Greg to go up on the outside balcony and rescue my shoe.

Tennis legend Jimmy Connors was a regular participant in the National Indoor Tennis Tournament that Billy brought to Memphis.

"Uncle Billy always did funny things like that to make my sister, my brother and I laugh. He's one of the funniest people I know, and I always enjoy the time I spend with him."

My nephew William Butler has always gotten the full brunt of my practical jokes:

"Uncle Billy always pranks me, putting whoopee cushions under my chair and sending me fake snakes in the mail. He always keeps me laughing, which is why I always looked forward to seeing him.

"When I hunt and fish with him, I never care about how many ducks we bag or how many fish we catch. I just love spending time with him. He really makes it fun while he's teaching me to be a real man and an outdoorsman.

"One time when his Suburban was in the shop, we took his Mercedes to go look at ducks at Quail Hollow. We crossed a flood-

ed ditch and the Mercedes got stuck in the mud, so we had to call his farmhands Mr. Wesley and Mr. Luke to come pull us out, which was hilarious.

"Uncle Billy has been a large influence in my life. I'm thankful I know him."

My niece and nephew just experience my pranks part of the time on visits. But if you lived in my household, as did my daughter Kelli, I could be a bit relentless sometimes. She'll never forget the phrase "calf rope":

"You're walking across the kitchen, the refrigerator is in view where you can almost taste the Capri Sun you're about to drink. Like a leopard stealthily honing in on a youthful gazelle, you begin your pursuit.

"You round the corner, get past the bar stools and suddenly you feel a painful pinching like no other feeling. You whip your head around wildly to see the predator that's holding you and it's Daddy!

"Laughing wildly, grabbing, he keeps saying, 'Say Calf Rope! Say Calf Rope!' If you said 'calf rope,' it was like saying 'uncle' and you were admitting defeat. I didn't like to lose, but that charley horse grip he had would make you want to do some deep South hollerin'."

I always loved someone who could gig me as much as I could gig them, like my late friend George Barley, who was in charge of the "Save the Everglades" program.

When George and I got together, we were like two kids playing pranks on each other. We short-sheeted each other's beds, put fish in each other's boots.

One time in Washington when we were staying in the same hotel, I noticed George had put his shoes outside his door for the hotel bellman to collect for shining. I intercepted the shoes, bought some shoes from Goodwill and put them outside of George's door.

George just laughed, then decided to order room service breakfast for 50 people, charged under my name and delivered to my room. He showed up for breakfast in his bathrobe, politely holding open the door for the conga line of waiters hauling in coffee, juice, eggs, bacon and every breakfast item on the menu.

Another time, George invited Tommie and me to his house in Florida for a turkey hunt, including a dinner party.

As we progressed through the cocktail hour, George indiscreetly kept calling us out of the room away from the rest of the guests several times, pretending he wanted to show us something.

But every time we re-entered the main room, it was like someone flipped a switch on the conversation. Everything was spoken in hushed tones.

Tommie and I started wondering what the hell was going on when George let us in on his gag. He had told the guests that I was a very hyper person who didn't like a lot of noise, and that Tommie was my psychologist. He told his guests that several times during the night, Tommie was going to take me to an adjoining room to medicate me.

Now, I know there were times when I must have done some crazy shit. I must have been a bad ass.

I'm also the same guy who couldn't toot a single note on that damned trumpet. But I was rather stunning in Kelli's bathing suit.

Of course now, I'm very mature. Well, sometimes. Some people calling it "pacing themselves." I call it "selective maturity."

LONG-TERM INTEREST RATES DIVE TO 7%: PAGE MW10

ALAN ABELSON • 3
Where not to find signs of intelligent life

THE INTERVIEW • 18
Extending the charge of the aging bull

ECONOMIC BEAT • 34
Are we heading toward recession?

BARRON'S

THE DOW JONES BUSINESS AND FINANCIAL WEEKLY

MAY 8, 1995 $3.00

Cotton King

Cotton prices have surged higher than they've been since the Civil War, and no one is happier about it than William "Billy" Dunavant, the tycoon who moves cotton markets worldwide. A look inside his secretive empire. Page 25

In 1995, *Barron's* magazine named Billy the "Cotton King" — "the man who moves cotton markets worldwide."

---------- 11 ----------

The Knack

IN THE COTTON BUSINESS, I HAD THE KNACK. I WAS really good at knowing when to buy and when to sell. It was just gut instinct.

If I had been in the lumber business, it might have not been the same, but I wasn't in the lumber business. I was in the cotton business.

My Daddy always told me – and I totally agree with him – timing was the reason for success and failure. If you used good timing, you'd win 95 percent of the time. Bad timing and you'd be out of business pretty quick. But we were blessed, really blessed.

He taught me to structure for success by hiring the best people we could find, like hiring Clarence Bowe and moving him to Phoenix in 1959 to run our Arizona operation, and hiring Sam Reeves who moved to Fresno in 1965 to oversee our California operations.

Clarence was just a good guy who could deal with anybody. One time, he made friends with the chief of a Hopi Indian reservation in Arizona. He made a deal for us to buy all their cotton for about five years.

We never had a losing season in either Arizona or California. I trusted they would do their jobs, because it allowed me to do mine.

Clarence had such faith in me that he sent me something via Telex that he entitled "New Company Poem." It went like this with each of the nine letters of my last name cleverly beginning a sentence:

D oing business with us is must.
U nder rules from the top you can trust.
N ever worry when W.B.D. gives you a market tip.
A lways listen when he says, "It may dip."
V ictory has always been his ultimate goal.
A nd believe me he will never end up in the hole.
N ot everyone knows this man's burning desire.
T o suceeed and to stay out of the fire.

Feedback from our employees, maybe not necessarily as creative as Clarence's poem, was important to me. So when we moved our offices from Front Street to Getwell in 1971 when we formed Dunavant Enterprises Inc., we built a dining room and we started having executive lunches.

We were growing and building, so why not have a dining room where you could have your key people in for lunch? We learned a lot from that little dining room.

Two or three days a week, we would have guests. Some contributed to the business and others were just guests as we exchanged business ideas.

I knew how to fill up a day. I was very organized in that structure of knowing what to do during the day, because I was busy all the time. I seemed to always have something to do, and I got it all done.

What you get out of life depends on how much you put in it. That was a natural, God-given talent. I utilized mine.

I was a real optimist. I would have never gotten in the cotton industry if I hadn't been an optimist.

Maybe my optimism led me to being a risk-taker, though I never realized how much risk I was taking daily.

I enjoyed taking risks because I enjoyed winning. As I accumulated risk, I never stepped back and said, "Billy, you've got too big a position on, you're going to lose money."

Forward contracting was my best claim to fame.

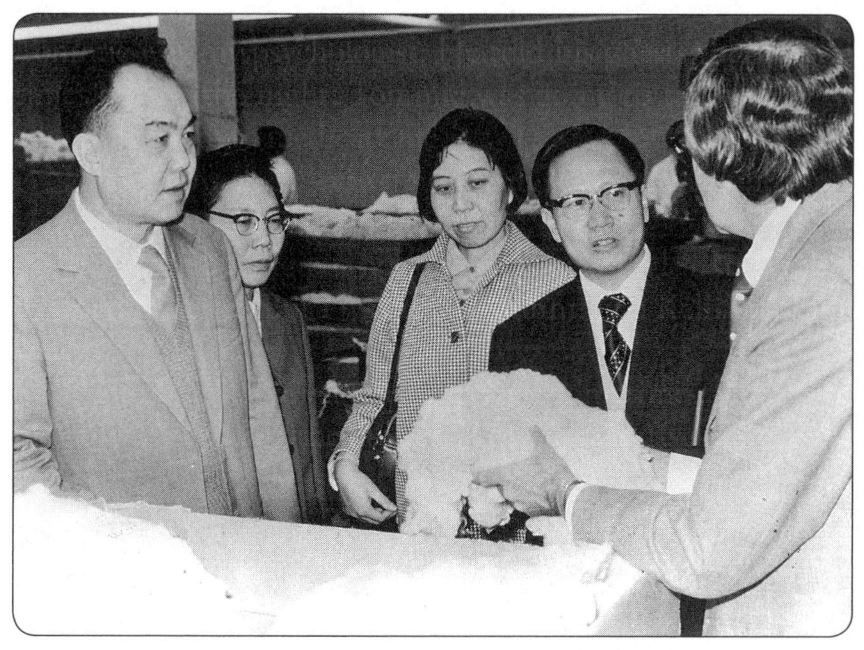

Negotiations with China gave Billy his well-deserved reputation as the King of Cotton.

A farmer plants his cotton today and he can sell it and deliver next December. You give him the price. Sometimes you can do it on call. If he thinks the price is going up, he can fix the price later. You can hedge.

There were three or four different terms. One was to buy everything at one price, and there were two or three other contracts that had stipulations in them.

The farmers loved it, because it was weighted toward them, not me. The risk was greater on me than them. It worked 8 out of 10 times.

All my competitors said it was too risky. And I agreed with them. So they didn't do it. Eight out of 10 is pretty good odds, but most people thought it would be 1 out of 10.

But if you were in control of what you did, you had a lot better mastery of what you were doing. We learned how to hedge

Almost every Saturday afternoon, Billy's dad Buck Dunavant could be found skeet shooting at the Memphis Skeet and Gun Club with his friends.

ourselves as we went along the trail. When we saw negatives, we tried to shore those things up.

I also created shipping gin direct, which means we'd ship the cotton directly from the ginner to the mill, which would reduce warehouse costs.

We had no competition for the first four or five years. And we never had a lot of competition because it was too friggin' risky.

But we were Dunavant Enterprises. People wanted to do business with us as one of my young friends Coleman Connell recalls:

"My father and grandfather each had a cotton farm in Mississippi. Billy had the deal that he would buy your cotton from

you at a fixed price and there was an escalator clause that if the market went up he'd give you half the gains.

"It was a no-brainer. There was no way to pass up that deal. His competition had no chance to buy a bale. My father was explaining to his father what Billy was doing. My grandfather, who was also a cotton merchant, said, 'You've got to be kidding me. Get Billy on the phone and I want to listen.'

"So using two phones sitting across from each other, Daddy called Mr. D while my grandfather listened. He said, 'I want you to explain it again, go through it again.' Mr. D went through it in 60 seconds. My father agreed on the phone to sell him his cotton and it was the first time my father didn't sell his crop to my grandfather. While my father was still on the phone with Mr. D, my grandfather said, 'Send him my company's cotton, too.'"

I never felt I had to outwork anybody. It was just my nature. I guess I thought I knew what to do and I did it. Getting the deal done was my mantra, and each day was a new challenge. I hardly ever looked back, as Paul Tudor Jones, my cousin and one of the world's top financial managers, remembers:

"Billy's business acumen was a combination of great self-confidence and even greater vision.

"While always looking ahead, he was able to have the self-confidence to acknowledge his mistakes while not dwelling on them to where it would hinder his progression both intellectually and from an aptitude standpoint. It allowed him to keep his forward-thinking vision.

"If you think about Billy in terms of a military commander, he was like Patton, because he was always moving forward. Patton used to say, 'A good plan, violently executed now, is better than a perfect plan next week."

"I'd put Billy in that forward category. He brought this huge energy level that kept the entire organization moving forward.

When he'd make mistakes, he'd acknowledge but not dwell on them.

"He is always four or five steps ahead of the competition, always thinking about X number of moves, X number of months ahead in the markets as opposed to what was happening in the here and now.

"As a trader, he was just spectacular. He was very forward looking. And that's the mark of a great trader.

"He was crazy like a fox. His idea of forward trading is no different than what an option-maker would do on a very flaky option market. He was doing it by that internal calculator. All forward trading was simply a trading option pricing for something way out in the future. But no option model could have ever priced that accurately.

"His combination of this incredible in-the-moment quickness, quick wit, quick thinking, his extreme emotional investment, whether it was anger or tears, and that combination of present moment self-awareness plus extraordinary forward thinking and vision, made him the guy with one of the greatest 'it' factors of anyone I've ever known in my business career or any friend that I've ever had.

"Billy is something else."

I sure did like the cotton business. I really thought I knew it, and I did know it. I also made lots of mistakes in it. In 1976, I forward contracted for about a million acres of cotton, but bad weather cut the volume so badly that I took my biggest loss ever (about $30 million) until 2004 when I lost money because China didn't keep its word. I was also in the wrong place at the wrong time, just bad timing.

Fortunately during my career, it didn't happen much. Looking back, it means a lot to me that I had the respect of some of my fiercest competitors such as Joe Nicosia, whom I once offered a job:

"There was only one King of Cotton and it was Billy Dunavant. It fits him to a 'T.' There's a special place for people who earn things all by themselves, who took an opportunity and built it.

"The amount of pride you have – you can't do it without some level of ego, but you don't have ego if you don't have something to back it up, and he could back it up.

"When you're a success, it's a product of your hard work, your intelligence and you've got to be a bit lucky as everybody is. But you don't re-cut the mold. There isn't another one that comes up behind you. There's a reason why Billy was so successful, because he was special.

"I'm not so sure the important part of that is not looking back. I think the hard part is making the decision. He had no problem ever making a decision. The worst thing you can ever do is not make a decision. It's okay to be right, it's okay to be wrong, it's not okay to not have an opinion, not in our business.

"Our business is a keep-score game. We keep score. Your profits and losses are the final score. And you can't do that without making decisions.

"One of Billy's strengths was his ability to take the facts he knew, analyze where he thought he had an advantage and come to a sufficient conclusion so he could make a decision to move forward.

"The one thing I can remember early in my career is the world started to change in commodity trading. In the 1980s, it was all about what the large commercials were doing, because they were driving the business. If you were in our business, there was only one thing you wanted to know – it was what is Billy doing, what is Billy thinking. Whether he was giving a speech or whether he was talking to a broker or whether you were talking with somebody who knew Billy second-hand, first-hand, what you wanted to know is what he knew."

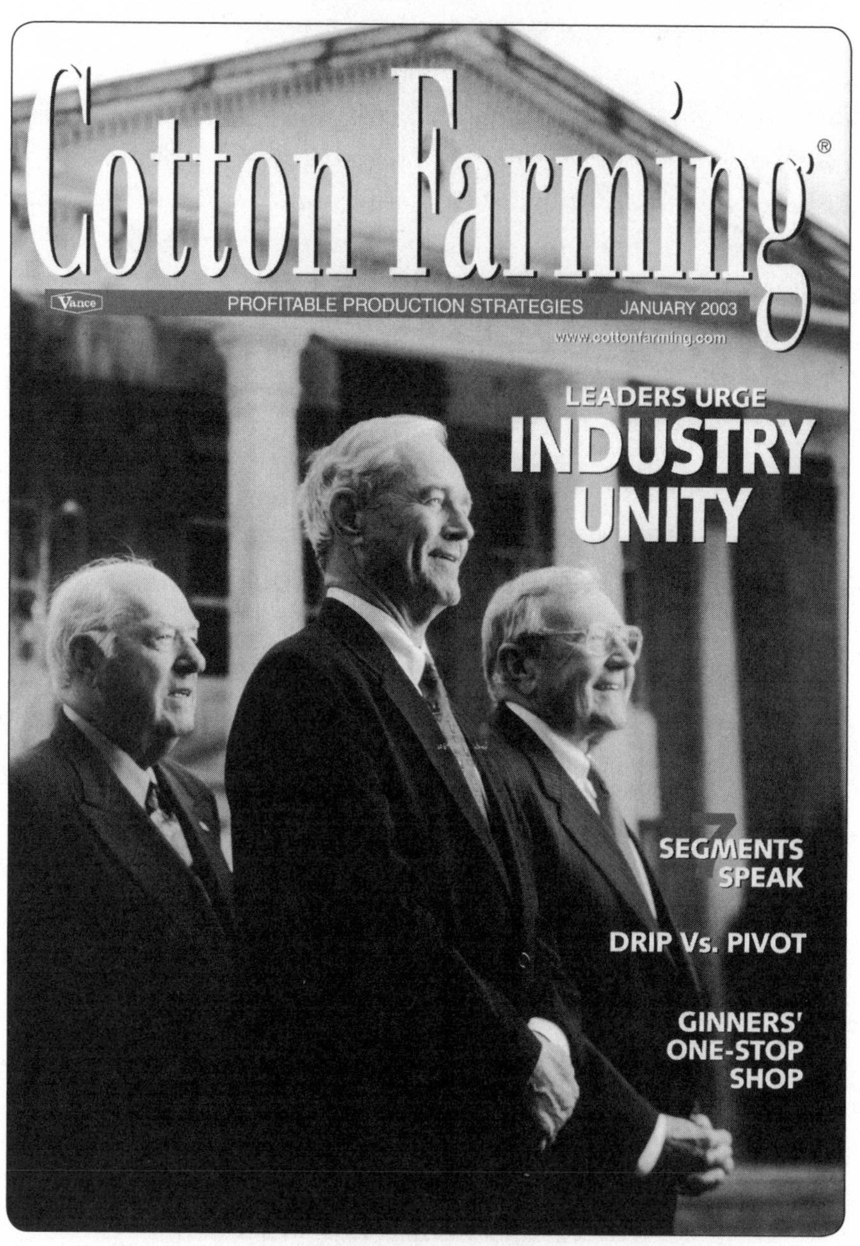

The January 2003 issue of *Cotton Farming* magazine featured the leaders of the cotton industry: Duke Kimbrell, Ken Hood, and Billy Dunavant.

We probably could have sat there and made money just doing cotton. But diversifying into other areas and investments was a way I thought we could grow the business.

We made a lot of money storing and shipping cotton. We also had divisions such as the Dunavant Exports Corporation, which made a commission on export sales as well as Dunavant Financial Inc., which handled trading in foreign currency futures on the international money market.

I made sure all my divisions were kept financially separate so I could see who was toeing the line and who wasn't.

Were all the divisions and diversifications the right way to build a multimillion-dollar business that spanned the globe? I don't know what else I would have done or we could have done to grow the business to that extent without taking some of these satellite risks.

As we grew, real estate was a logical acquisition. If we paid too much, we knew it would grow into that in time. It has been a very lucrative part, it's a good hedge, but it ties up lots of your capital.

The first major real estate I bought were cotton warehouses in Memphis. It was logical because it fit our business, as our Dunavant Enterprises attorney Russ Cherry recalls:

"If you're using warehouses that you don't own, information gets out quick. But if you own your warehouses, you own your brokerage company and everything is kept in house. People aren't aware when you're making these big moves. That led us into the real estate, one thing led into another and we kept it all in house.

"With the cotton business, what Boss (Billy) was trading on was to be able to make moves that influenced the market without anybody knowing what he was doing. So that's why he kept a lot of these side subsidiaries and set them up so that he could move quickly, efficiently and secretly, because that's how it's traded.

"These other businesses that he was into, especially real estate, had always been a hedge. A trader's mentality is to always hedge. Even when the market got funny and went south, we still had real estate. It was solid and now we're beginning to sell what we want to sell.

"It was a safe hedge, which is completely different probably from what most people would do. But Boss was always concerned about what happens if. As it turned out, it's one of the smartest things he ever did.

"Traders, sometimes if they've got a lot of cash, continue to put cash into a position. Boss was always smart to get out. He knew when to call it quits, cut it off and go. That's his trader's mentality. He's applied that to all of his other businesses. If a company is not making money, stop.

"A classic example is we had a furniture factory that was making luggage in Hartsville, Tennessee, north of Lebanon. It sat at the base of what was going to be the Hartsville nuclear reactor until the environmental people stopped it.

"We had a manufacturing facility, a furniture factory next to those big towers. It went for about two years and was losing money.

"So Billy calls the board of directors meeting and shareholders, and promptly fires everybody. Before he calls it, he has the chief financial officer put me on an airplane, fly there, rent a car, and show up at the factory office unannounced.

"I'm there to take the keys to the place, to take the cash and to tell 275 people that are out there making luggage that 'you've got to leave.'

"In the meantime, the guys from the cotton company trucking have tractor-trailers en route so we could pick up the finished luggage in the warehouse. If you didn't do that, it would have walked off. Then on top of $2 million of luggage, you had probably another $1 million in raw materials of things you could sell on the market like leather and vinyl.

"That's an example of when Boss makes a decision, he's done and he moves on to something else. That's how it's done.

"He always liked these different businesses that he never got intimately involved with. That's what he had other people do. He just traded, but he applied his trader's mentality and psyche to everything he did."

We often tried to get a foot in the door to develop something. It wasn't always the right thing to be doing.

We had a gold mine that I bought in Costa Rica. You don't start out to buy a gold mine in Costa Rica. It just developed in negotiations for whatever you were doing. The opportunity came forward and you said, well maybe it would help the other relationships if you buy one. You watch what you paid for it.

Now all I got out of that gold mine in Costa Rica was a hunk of pure gold. But that mine opened a lot of doors.

There was also the time that a Kentucky coal mine owned by Kentucky highway patrolmen became available. They came to us, presented us with a proposition and it sounded so good that we thought we'd get our money back in two weeks.

We put a couple million dollars into that mine, but it didn't work out. We lost a little money, not much, because the coal business was shutting down pretty quick. What we were in was the good part and the bad part was shutting down. We got our money back from the good side of what we did.

We had quite a few of those things in my lifetime, such as investing in the development in the world Golf Hall of Fame in St. Augustine, Florida. The Hall of Fame was profitable in time. All of them are and have been profitable in time. But a number of them we bought weren't profitable from the day we bought them and we understood that.

There's this hotel in Destin I own called the Henderson Beach Inn. Our real estate division found it. It was the only piece of property left in the Destin area that had really great beach frontage. We paid big-time for the beach frontage, but that's okay. The Henderson Beach National Park is to the right of it, and it can never be developed.

That little ol' inn makes about $1 million a year. It's very profitable, but it's not what we're destined to do. We've got to have something much bigger than that to pay the debt. So we're investing $300 million to add another 171-room hotel that will have 10,000 square feet of indoor space including ballrooms and 30,000 square feet of outdoor space for group functions. We're also thinking about adding another 95-room hotel and 200 luxury condos. We are aiming for completion in spring 2016.

I've always liked to develop stuff, but I sure did like the cotton business. I had a lot more good visions than bad visions in it. I really knew that business.

In 1973, Billy reigned as King of the Memphis Cotton Carnival.

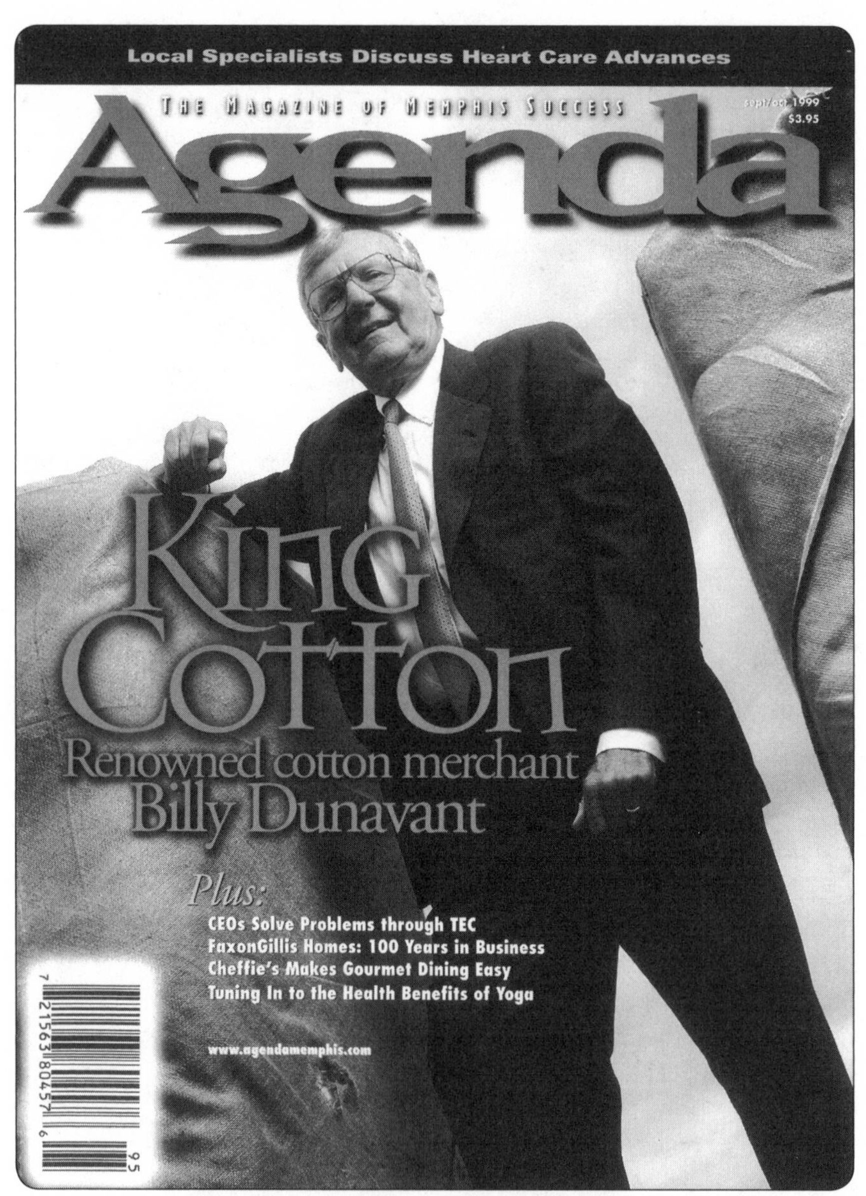

Billy was not only a leader in the worldwide cotton industry but also a leader in the Memphis business community.

12

Bossman

I'VE OFTEN BEEN ASKED WHY I WAS FORTUNATE enough to be successful at such a high level for a long time.

You just read many of those reasons in the previous chapter.

The one element I can't emphasize enough is hiring people who are the very best at what they do, letting them do their jobs and holding them accountable if they don't.

When I thought about hiring people, it was more than just hiring an employee. It was like I was hiring someone to join our family.

Here are some of the people I've hired through the years, and what they think about me. It's interesting for me to read their observations for the first time:

H.J. Weathersby, Dunavant Enterprises treasurer: *"Cotton was the mainstay, but all the other things that Billy dabbled in made life at Dunavant very interesting.*

"We were in the chicken business, in the gold business, in the coal business, in the waterslides business in South Texas, USFL football, World Basketball League basketball, just to name a few. We owned Memphis Aero for a number of years and ran that operation.

"We got into a bunch of different stuff. Was it all profitable? No. But it reduced the monotony of coming to work every day and just buying and selling cotton, which was Billy's expertise and something he did very well.

"There was always something going on. Billy just liked making deals. He made quick decisions. He could sum up the situation quickly and he was right many more times than he was wrong.

"We learned quickly when to get out of a deal. We bought a coal mining business when coal was selling for $120 a ton. We were making money hand over fist. About six months after we bought it, it dropped to like $60 a ton. Rather than making money, we were going to lose our rear end. We couldn't get out of the coal business fast enough.

"Billy was demanding. When he wanted your undivided attention, and when he wanted something, he wanted it now, not tomorrow.

"You understood that, but he was always fair. When he told you he was going to do something, he did it.

"I've been with Dunavant Enterprises for 39 years, working toward retiring completely in about another year before I work as a consultant for Billy. It has been a very good relationship, an unforgettable journey. I traveled around the world, got to go to a lot of great places for Billy. I've enjoyed working for him."

Steve Ehrhart, executive director of the AutoZone Liberty Bowl and former general manager of the Showboats: *"If anything, Billy is a triple-A personality. He goes at 'Dunavant' speed. He's had more speeding tickets than I care to comment about. You always want to be early with Billy. There's no Dunavant time and real time. He has the same speed when he hunts and fishes. It's full speed ahead. He's the Energizer Bunny.*

"He lives life at a very full stage. His friend John Dobbs once told him, 'Dunavant, you know how to enjoy your life and enjoy your money. I've got to figure out how to do what you do. I've got to figure out a way to live at this full-speed life.'

"Billy can process information quickly because of his photographic memory. In his head he knew all the moving parts of international cotton and how many bales are here and there and

at what price. His brilliance of being able to analyze fast and make quick decisions was why he was so successful in everything he took on.

"When he was trying to make the decision to have an operation in Australia, some guys came up from Australia to see Billy. They had worked for weeks to put together this elaborate proposal. They figured it would take a couple of days to present it.

"They get in Billy's office and after about the first 15 minutes, Billy said, 'Okay.' The guys kept right going. Billy said, 'Did you hear me? I said, 'Okay.' They kept right on going because they couldn't believe it. Finally he said, 'If you keep going, I'm going to change my mind. We're doing it. Now get out of here.'

"Making quick decisions is something I learned from him while building the Showboats. We wanted to sign linebacker John Corker. I explained to Billy that Corker had some off-the-field problems. Billy said, 'Just make your decision and go.'

"Billy is not going to let the grass grow while making a decision. Once he gets going down a certain way, he goes.

"Billy is very tuned into kids. It's why his grandkids love him. The first time he met my son Brandon, my son was 9 years old and wearing a watch.

"Billy started a conversation with Brandon and asked, 'You want to sell that watch? How much you want for it?' Brandon ended up selling it to him for like $12. Brandon credits that now in his career of being able to make decisions.

"Billy, being a consummate trader, said, 'Yeah, I was trying to teach him the values of being a merchant and a trader, not just small talk. You have to think and apply what's my watch worth and what would I sell it for?'

"Fair is a huge word with Billy. He always wanted his people to be right with other people. It's why Billy is my boss, my mentor, my role model. He inspires people to really do well."

Billy with sons (l-r) Buck, Bill III, and John.

Ansel Davis, who worked as a Dunavant Enterprises attorney and now manages country artists such as Keith Urban in Nashville: *"There are many people in life who give you a helping hand, but a few of them are the ones that change who you are. The opportunity Billy gave me changed my life immeasurably.*

"I worked for him from 1977 to 1983. That doesn't seem long, but it was like a 24-hour-a-day job. A friend of mine once said, 'It's not how old you are; it's how long you've been awake.' It wasn't 24 hours a day with Billy, but it kind of was. Six years was kind of like 12.

"I couldn't wait to get to the office because you never knew what was going to happen next.

"When I was hired by Billy, it was just my third job after graduating from the University of Kentucky law school in 1974.

"I had taken over my father-in-law's practice outside St. Louis for six months because he underwent open-heart surgery. To take over a middle-aged guy's practice right out of law school was pretty exciting, so I wasn't looking for a new job.

"I was in Billy's daughter Connie's first wedding. I went down to Memphis for some Cotton Carnival parties. Connie said, 'My father is looking for a lawyer. You ought to go talk to him.'

"She mentions this on a Thursday morning and the next day she said, 'Dad can see you today if you want to go see him. He's looking for a lawyer. You really ought to go. I think y'all would like each other.'

"I didn't know anything about Billy or the cotton business, but I go to his office. I'm talking to him, but he also has two hardline phones going and somebody else is standing there talking to him.

"He's carrying on a conversation with all of them while interviewing me, if that's what he was doing. In the end, he hangs up all his calls, looks at me and says, 'Fine, when can you start? Never mind. Start Monday.' Then, he picked up the phone again.

"I said, 'Wait a minute. I've got a practice near St. Louis.'

"So we negotiated. The only negotiation we had was over how much time he'd give me before I had to start working for him. I wanted a month, he wanted 10 days and we finally agreed on two weeks as my start date.

"I'm staying with Connie and her then-husband at the time. She said, 'What happened?' I said, 'I think I got the job.' She said, 'Yeah, he called.' I said, 'Yeah Connie, it's interesting. I'm not going to go ask, but he didn't tell me what he was going to pay me or anything else. It was all over so fast.'

"So when I moved to Memphis and started working for Billy, I had no idea what I was getting paid.

"But when you get around Billy, you just know he's one of the most dynamic people you'll ever meet. I'm an only child, so going to work for him in the family atmosphere he creates is a little bit like being adopted.

"I was 27 years old when he hired me. All the other lawyers he talked to had a connection to somebody in Memphis, somebody's son or something. By hiring me, somebody from out-of-state, everybody was going to be mad or nobody was going to be mad.

"Billy gave me a job that I probably didn't deserve at the time, but I grew into it. Billy was like that – he'd throw you in the water and you could either swim or you couldn't. And he'd always back you.

"If you made a mistake, only you and he knew it. He would never disagree with you in front of somebody else. If you got scolded, it was just the two of you. Once he corrected the problem with you, he turned the card and it was a new day.

"It's a lesson he taught me that I've used when hiring employees. You associate yourself with talented people and give them the rope and let them run. They figure it out. You don't have to figure out who's the lead dog of the pack. They'll show you.

"Give them more responsibility, probably more than they actually deserve. If you give people a position of authority they only warrant and deserve at the time, you don't test them. Give them more, and you'll find out who the winners are. If you keep everybody in their comfort zone, then they'll do just what they are capable of.

"Billy did that time and time again. When Billy turns you loose, he turns you loose.

"When I got hired, I went home and did this crash course about the cotton business. I took two weeks – one week to get out of what I was doing there at that law firm and the next week to study the cotton business.

"The first day, I go in the office feeling like I know something about the cotton business. Billy says, 'We've got a plane waiting for you. I want you to go to Pikeville, Kentucky where we have a coal mine. Figure how to sell that damned thing.'

"He didn't tell me what to sell it for. He said, 'Sell it.' My family had been in the coal business.

"I told Billy, 'I don't know much about the coal business but I know more than you do and you own one.'

"I wish I had one of the characteristics Billy taught me, which is making a decision and never looking back. You make a decision with the best information you've got and you live with it until you realize you're wrong and you change it in a heartbeat. I've tried that and I've failed. I still look back and second-guess.

"Billy never second-guessed himself, he never looked back. He could also turn on a dime. If he made a decision, invested a lot of money and realized it was wrong, he'd walk away in a heartbeat.

"We set up one of the first commodity future trading companies on the Chicago exchange, and he invested millions in it. One day, Billy woke up and realized the downside risk. He called me in his office on a Monday or a Tuesday and said, 'How long would it take to liquidate every operation we have in Chicago?'

"I said, 'Hell, we just got into it 18 months ago.' He said, 'I want out by the weekend.' I said, 'I don't know how you can do that.' He said, 'I want out by the weekend. Whatever it takes, whoever it takes, I want out by the weekend.'

"Bob Zellar, who was running it, was arguing with Billy over the phone that he could liquidate it over a period of time. Billy said, 'My lawyer is coming up there. You see him and liquidate everything immediately. If you don't, he will.'

"Nobody would do that, but Billy figured out at that time that the downside was insane in that market.

"I worked for Billy when it was the best time to be in Memphis in the cotton business. Cotton was the king and Billy basically invented exporting and forward contracting.

"Looking back, it was pretty amazing. It was a worldwide operation, and I got there during a growth period when they were expanding into Japan and Australia in the late 1970s.

"Dunavant Enterprises grew a lot and got involved in ancillary businesses. The good thing about it was I was involved in setting some of those up.

"They got into everything. Off-shore supply boats, real estate, trucking, cotton warehouses and the coal business.

"Billy was a risk taker. In 10 years, he made his company one of the biggest in the world. That's Billy. He had just two speeds – stop and kill. He had more energy than anybody I've ever seen.

"He didn't need any chairs in his office. You never got to sit down. He had a trader's mentality. You didn't ever hand him a piece of paper because he wasn't going to read anything.

"All of the lengthy discussions I had with Billy took place standing at his desk usually while he was doing something else. But you knew he was paying attention, even though he was always on the phone trading cotton. He'd turn and give you an answer. You had to learn he was completely listening to you, though he wasn't necessarily looking at you.

"Billy taught you to cut down your presentations. He was such a quick study that you had to figure out the essence of what you wanted to present to him before you actually did it.

"A smart thing Billy did was have a business dining room for lunches. The lunch table seated eight people. Billy was always at the head of the table. If you were in town and you were at a certain level in the company, you were expected to be there.

"The reason was brilliant. It meant you had an hour with Billy Dunavant and all the other top people in his company every day. I don't know if I deserved to be there. Once I started getting invited to those lunches, I never went anywhere else to lunch.

"It was an opportunity of having one hour with Billy at a time when no cell phones existed and the meeting could only be interrupted by Billy's secretary. You had one uninterrupted hour daily with the senior executives. It was invaluable for me as general counsel.

"Billy loves people. I never met anybody who didn't like Billy Dunavant, even his competitors. He's big on family, and Billy was like a second father to me. When I first came to town, he took

me around and introduced me to all of his friends. I knew the fathers of people my age.

"How many CEOs of a company hire a 27-year-old lawyer and then take the trouble to take him around town and introduce him? He knew I wasn't from Memphis and he wanted me to know people. It helped me immeasurably.

"He'd do that time and again. He really cared about the people who worked for him. It wasn't just the business. He cared about the people.

"He was always excited. If you took him an idea, his initial reaction was always positive. Then, he'd think about it and make a decision. But his initial reaction was positive, he never immediately shot you down.

"Billy had tremendous power, but he never abused anybody or anything. He was very candid in what he was going to do. He never misdirected. He told you exactly what he thought what was going to happen.

"He's always had a love for life. Billy's life is divided into two pieces: duck hunting and waiting to get back to duck hunting. I thought sometimes his company was a way to fund his duck hunting.

"On Thursday or Friday in duck season, you always knew he was going duck hunting because you'd walk in his office and his dogs were already there.

"When I went duck hunting with Billy, I'd find myself watching Billy more than I'd watch the ducks. Billy is never more alive than he is in a duck blind. Most times duck hunting is semi-social with a lot of drinking. He is so focused and is so alive. Every little antenna is standing up.

"Any trip with him was fun. One time, Billy bought this new set of very expensive luggage. We were in New York and going to Geneva and on to London.

"His luggage had handles on it. It starts to go through an x-ray machine and security said they couldn't run it through because of the handles.

"Now, this is very expensive luggage and anybody else would have argued with them. Billy reached in his pocket, pulled out a pocketknife back in an era where security didn't care about that, cut all the handles off the luggage, looked at security and said, 'Now, are you happy?' Boom. Done. Never hesitated.

"I married a Nashville girl and all Nashville girls want to move back to Nashville, so I left Billy and became general counsel in the real estate syndication business when it was booming in Nashville.

"Eventually, I got to know Neil Diamond. Being a music lawyer looked like a lot of fun. Then I moved into music management.

"I miss being around Billy. He's like Halley's comet. There won't be another one."

Russ Cherry, Dunavant Enterprises attorney: *"Billy would have a board of directors meeting, everybody gives a boring report, he remembers the numbers and says, 'Okay, you better go and do it.' If they come back the next year and they haven't done it, he makes changes.*

"It's not like he micromanaged anybody. That wasn't his style. That still isn't his style.

"At those catered executive lunches we had in the office, you had to think about what you were doing, you had to be careful what you said because it was still work despite the presence of guests.

"All of a sudden, you'd get grilled on what about this or that. Someone might say, 'Well, I have to go research that.'

"I heard Billy tell a guy once, 'I understand that you don't know the answer, and you're going to research it and get back to me. But don't let it happen too many times, so I'll be wondering whether you're worth a damn or not.'

"He's very direct. What you see is what you get. He's very casual. He commands respect. If he told you something, he did it. If he didn't tell you, he wouldn't do it. He's sort of like the first lawyer I worked for. Don't make promises you can't keep. If someone does well, reward them. He's a very generous man."

Bill Dunavant, son, CEO and president of Dunavant Enterprises: *"Dad has been a lifetime mentor for me. His business integrity is still in me to the bone, even though the integrity of the industry today isn't like it used to be when a handshake was gold.*

"It was phenomenal the way Dad timed his business career and kept his hunger for the next deal and the next deal and the next deal.

"He surrounded himself with incredibly bright people, and they all bought into the teamwork.

"Dad all made us feel important, but he was clearly the leader always. His decisions were crisp and they were damned well always right.

"He was brilliant in his timing, brilliant in the market. It was great having a leader that was 10 steps ahead of everybody.

"He thrived in a high-pressure, high-intensity world. It was his drug. He loved the pressure, he loved the stress, he loved the art of the next deal. He was driven like nobody I've ever known.

"Dad was never afraid to let you fail just so you learned from your mistakes. Sometimes, the wins aren't as important as why you lost. What did you learn from it?

"There's nobody who could cuss you and make you feel as bad as he could make you feel about a mistake. But five minutes later he's moved to something else. You may have a scar from that chewing, but that scar healed pretty quickly because the lesson was learned.

"I came to work for Dad in 1982, straight after graduating from the University of Virginia. My first job was in the ware-

The 2008 Board of Directors of Dunavant Enterprises.

house. Dad said, 'If you're going to work for me you're going to start at the bottom.' I appreciated that. It made sense, because it instilled the sense of values that I still carry today.

"After that start, I traveled around the United States for him before posting up in Japan. I really enjoyed the international side of business. I went to Australia and fell in love with it. Dad said he wasn't going to move there, but also said, 'If you want to build an operation there, go build it.' I was the most traveled guy ever back and forth to Australia. We built a big operation in Australia that was successful.

"Our company leaders around the United States and the world had the autonomy to make their decisions and run their businesses. Dad picked his teammates carefully and they were all very capable. He gave them the tools to be successful and there's no guy that wanted everybody in the company to be successful more than

Dad. He wanted everybody to be as successful as him, because his success bred success for others.

"I saw he wanted everybody to be proud of our wins and our success. When we all failed, we all heard about it, but that's just the way it was.

"In his history-making China deals, I was fortunate to be next to him along with David Hardoon, who ran our Asian operations, to watch Dad and David execute these megasales that had to be kept quiet for three to four weeks. Those were epic business lessons to experience, as was the great work that was done in Geneva and in South Africa by Rickard Laurin and his team where they put together a business model that was sustainable and gave back to the community.

"It has been an incredible ride to be with Dad, to witness his generosity, to see what he has been able to give back to the community, to see the way he operated with a great team of people executing the plan.

"There has been no greater honor to be his son, work by his side and follow him in his business."

Woodson Dunavant, son, director of global sales, Dunavant Enterprises: *"I grew up in the sample room and came in the company in 2001. By that time, my older brothers were already in the company and established. I had to find my niche where I would fit in. Dad would keep up with what I was doing via other employees. The challenges were not to let him down, to learn the business and do well.*

"I was lucky to come into the business straight out of college. He let me travel the world. I lived in Hong Kong for a year, in Geneva and Europe for a year. I lived for six months in Australia. Just the opportunity to travel the globe and learn the business was all because of him. All my brothers did the exact same thing. The fact I could do that was just an absolute blessing.

"The bottom line was he was the boss and if I screwed up he'd call me in his office. If I ever did anything well, he'd pat me on the back, which didn't happen very often. To get a compliment out of him you'd have to do something real right. But as long as I wasn't being called in for doing bad things, then I thought I was doing a decent job.

"His timing of trading in the market was impeccable. He knew when to get out of a bad trade and he knew when to get in when something good was about to happen.

"It's sort of a sixth sense. I guess I have it, but I've never used it in trading. I use it in reading people. I can tell within 10 to 15 minutes of meeting somebody whether they are a good person by their facial expressions and hand gestures.

"That's a trait I feel like I picked up from Dad.

"The daily executive lunches were special, especially when we had guests like (then-Memphis basketball) Coach (John) Calipari. Watching Dad and Cal interact was really something to see, because those are two Alphas with so much respect for one another."

John Dunavant, son, senior vice-president of Dunavant Enterprises: *"I couldn't have worked for a better person, the leader of the cotton industry who happened to be my father.*

"There was pressure being his son working in his company, but I wouldn't say it was elevated. He was pretty consistent with the way he treated all his employees. Being one of his sons, we probably interacted with him more than other employees, so we were apt to get more ass-chewings at times. I needed my butt kicked and it kept me straight most of the time. He taught me that persistence pays off.

"When he retired, it took awhile for him to flip the switch and turn it off. It's that way for most people, but even more so for someone like him who had the daily stress of trading futures and options.

"I think he finally learned to appreciate other things outside of the cotton business and started enjoying retirement."

Buck Dunavant, son, CEO of Arthur Dunavant Investments and former vice-president of Dunavant Enterprises: *"I do the same thing Dad did. He was a physical trader of cotton, but he made his money speculating in the market.*

"When I was a kid, I didn't know what 9:30 (a.m.) meant, I didn't know that it's when the market opened for trading. I just knew at 9:30 we needed to be near a phone, no matter where we were. We might be standing on the side of the road in Vernon, Texas, at some bebop stop with a pay phone. He'd hand me a $100 bill and say, 'Start getting me quarters.' All I did was feed the pay phone.

"Over the years, I kept wondering, 'Damn, what was this deal about 9:30?'

"Then when I was a freshman in high school, Dad took me and some of my friends to the New York Board of Trade. We went down and watched that 9:30 opening on the floor. There was an adrenalin rush watching 50 guys screaming at the top of their lungs filling orders for Dad. Turns out three of the four people on that trip became commodity traders.

"I'm an adrenalin junkie like my Dad was. My Dad was addicted to making money, that's what he did. I always wanted to follow in his footsteps in futures and options. There's where I gravitated to and Dad was kind enough to let me work under him. As he got older and was traveling, he'd call me and have me execute the futures and options for him. I took a great deal of pride in it, but I also took a real interest in it, because it was truly an adrenalin rush. It still is.

My Dad was a great athlete growing up and I played sports as well. The one thing I still like to know at the end of the day in business is whether I win or lose. And in Dad's business of trading futures and options, every day at 1:15 the whistle sounded and the scoreboard showed whether he won or lost.

"That's what I enjoyed most about working with Dad. He was the most intense guy you'll ever meet. He could make people nervous. Many times he asked someone a question though he already knew the answer. The absolute worst thing you could do was bullshit him on an answer. Dad didn't tolerate dummies.

"Dad hired people that were smarter than him in areas that he had no interest. He'd hire a CFO like Louis Baioni and he trusted Louis and he knew Louis was as smart as him.

"Once Dad hired you and trusted you, he gave you as much rope as you needed. But he held you accountable. If you screwed up, he'd be on your ass about it.

"I'm probably more like Dad than any of my brothers. I've got a bad temper that I probably got from him. I consider myself very competitive, but my Dad is the most competitive person I've ever known. Even today, I feel my Dad still wants to compete.

"At our house, we have several quotes we live by. One of them is 'The lead sled dog has the best view.' Dad had always been No. 1 in everything and I hope that everything I do I do 100 percent. That is something Dad has instilled in me.

"That's the way Dad has lived his life. He has always been the leader and he wasn't willing to be second fiddle. I have the drive my Dad has. You can't teach that.

"You can't teach instinct and Dad was a great trader because he was instinctive. Sure, he studied the market but Dad had remarkable instincts.

"What made him exceptional in the cotton market is when he was wrong about a trade, he got out of it. He was gone. The first loss was the best loss. He was so damned good at cutting his losses right off the bat.

"Dad was very good at holding people accountable, but he was the first one to admit it when he screwed up."

Louis Baioni, Dunavant Enterprises treasurer and partner: *"Billy was in the process of forming Dunavant Enterprises when he asked me, 'Do you want the job?' I said, 'Yes, I do'. It has been a great 31 years with Billy.*

"His integrity hasn't changed from day one, and neither did his work ethic. He would never think about screwing someone out of a deal. He was a tough negotiator. But it was always above board.

"His word is his bond. He never deviated from that. He always had the uncanny ability of having total focus on whatever he was doing, whether it was business or hunting or playing tennis."

Rickard Laurent, former manager of Dunavant Enterprises European operations in Geneva, Switzerland: *"I worked 32 years for Billy Dunavant and it was a very fantastic time. The work and the money were obviously good, but what stays with you is all the people I met around the world.*

"I had worked for Borje Johannson with a cotton company in Fresno, California, called Cook Industries. In 1978 when the company shut down, Billy contacted Borje, who had been with Cook for 22 years, and said, 'Borje, please don't take another job before you talk to me.'

"Borje was a hot commodity in those days because he was an expert on China. Billy had already done the first China business but Borje was involved in that as well. After six months, Borje called Billy and went to see him.

"You know Billy. He made him an offer he thought he could not possibly refuse to become general manager of Dunavant Enterprises' Far East operation. And Borje said, 'Thank you very much. Let me go home and sleep on this, talk to my wife and I'll give you an answer tomorrow.'

"That wasn't Mr. Dunavant's idea of business. He said, 'I want a decision now.' He supposedly doubled the offer and Borje took the job.

"I talked to Borje and said, 'I can take a job setting up the company for Dunavant in Geneva.' I had to open an office there for Cook Industries two years earlier, so I had done this.

"I made a budget of $100,000, including my salary, a secretary, office, travel, telex, fax, everything. I went to see Mr. Dunavant and said, 'You are a fairly wealthy man so if this doesn't work out for you I think you can manage. I'm a young man, so that's not a big problem either. Should we try?'

"That was how I started to work for Billy Dunavant, first named as general manager of European merchandising and sales.

"It was basically a sales office at the start. After not much more than a year, I told Billy, 'It will cost you money having this office if you don't let me trade.' Then we started slow and we went from one thing to the next.

"He was a great risk taker. He'd go in heavily at times. The way I perceived it if he saw it wasn't working he'd get out quickly with a small loss or break even, then sit back and wait for the next opportunity.

"When he didn't like a deal, he said, 'Why don't we do half?' This was his way of saying 'I'm not 100 percent sure of this.' He was very astute. He studied people and understood people quite well.

"I learned to make many business decisions. I'd be wrong from time to time but if you did your due diligence and had good reason for acting the way you did, Billy was very soft and understanding about it. He wanted to solve your problem.

"I was at the board meeting in Memphis in the 1990s and I was talking about 'my company' in Geneva. Billy interrupted me and said, 'Rickard, you know it's my company, don't you?' I said, 'Yes, I do, I know very well it's your company. But if I think and care about it like it's mine, you should be very happy.'"

David Hardoon, former manager of Dunavant Enterprises Far East operations in Hong Kong: *"I was working for Weil Brothers Cotton in Montgomery, and they sent me after a year's training to run their Asian and Pacific operations when Billy decided to make me an offer I couldn't refuse. I guess he offered me because I was a pain in his side.*

"He brought me to Memphis in 1985, booked us a private room at Justine's and within an hour laid out the deal which included a stipulation that I wouldn't start working for him for another year while Weil Brothers found a replacement for me.

"Compared to working for Weil Brothers, which was a very old and conservative firm, it was like night and day going to work for Billy.

"I was entrusted to merchandise Asian cotton, Indian cotton and Chinese cotton, but there was daily pressure because Billy was in the market every day.

"The most difficult thing was to be the first person if possible to get accurate information that would influence the market and at the same time to allow Billy to act on it.

"So it's one issue to sell cotton, but it's another issue to give Billy a perspective of what's going on in Asia in terms of crop reports, what governments were wanting to do, interpreting consumption and production numbers and talking to individual textile mills.

"Billy was ultra-competitive. He did have an explosive temper. I've listened at 2 a.m. on a speakerphone in Hong Kong when he was back in his office in Memphis using the harshest language you can imagine chewing out an employee. But when the storm is over, it's over.

"Yet he's very caring. He's a very generous, warm, emotional person. He was almost like an uncle to many employees. He hired you to do a job and he had confidence you could do the job.

"His company was structured on a geographical basis with different people like myself taking care of various parts of the world.

We all had a little fiefdom in which we operated in the parameters we were given.

"In the business of commodity trading, there's a lot of people with egos, especially if it's a privately owned company. But the thing about Billy was when he was winning, he considered the guy losing on the other side of the market. Billy was never the type of guy who would squeeze you until you were dead.

"Time and again, he would let you out. That is a testimony to his character."

Karen Rhoads, Dunavant Enterprises New York Cotton Exchange buyer/seller: *"I got a clerical job in Dunavant Enterprises back office in New York after trying college for a couple of months. I then was moved to the trading floor and after a couple of months, Mr. Dunavant said, 'She's staying on the trading floor, she's not going back.'*

"I ended up staying 34 years on the floor, dealing with Billy on a daily basis. I helped train all of his sons in the business.

"When I first started working on the floor, Mr. Dunavant used to play tennis every day at lunchtime in Memphis, regardless if the market was busy or not. He instructed me to call him if the market moved 50 points either way. If that happened, I'd call him whether he was on the tennis court or in the shower.

"He was great at what he did and he definitely was a fireball. There were days I told him I deserved combat pay.

"We had a specific phone line for Mr. Dunavant. Some days, he would be so crazy, his phone line would ring and we'd say to each other, 'You answer it, he likes you better.'

"He'd get mad at the market. You couldn't take it personally, like he was mad at you. You had to get over it. You had to learn to let it go. But it did take a couple of years to get used to it.

"Some days, we'd joke about it. Other days, I'd go home upset.

"One day, Mr. Dunavant and I got in an argument. I went home and said, 'I'm not going to talk to that man until tomor-

row.' He called me a few minutes later and said, 'You didn't call me with the five-minutes-before call.' I said, 'Yeah, I think I'm kind of mad at you. I've been home long enough to drink a bottle of wine.' He said, 'Your biggest mistake is you should have drank two bottles.'

"He always came up with great phrases. One time, there was this person he didn't like and he said, 'He couldn't sell dog shit in a circus.' When he called people 'Dickhead,' I had to explain to those people it meant he liked them.

"He always told me, 'You're my eyes and ears on the trading floor. I trust you 100 percent. In anything goes wrong, you've got to let me know.'

"Sometimes on that trading floor, you could have been a little bit crooked. I had to tell Mr. Dunavant when people were doing some bad stuff.

"People I associated with on the trading floor, even to this day, say Mr. Dunavant was a class act. He was a real good businessman who truly cared about people.

"We had an office in Tower 1 of the World Trade Center when 9/11 hit. We all made it out safe, but Mr. Dunavant was so upset because there was no cell service. It took awhile to track down everybody.

"Then he would call me daily. He was willing to do anything for you and he's still the same way.

"Even to this day when I talk to him, he says, 'If there is anything I can ever do for you please let me know.'

"I truly enjoyed working for him. We did have a special connection. He always teases me saying, 'You were my favorite employee.' He has been a very important part of my life. I miss him to death."

Joe Castleman, Billy's former pilot for almost 35 years: *"Billy ran on the clock. If he told you we were leaving at a certain time, that's when we left. Anybody who arrived late who was sup-*

posed to travel with us was left behind, like his kids on occasion. They'd be waving at us while we were taxiing out and we'd just take off.

"I flew Billy all over the world, including two or three times around the world on 30-day trips on which he visited all his international offices.

"We made so many interesting trips to places like China, Africa and Australia. There were some perks, like staying in the nicest hotels and eating the best food.

"But landing in some places, like in countries that had no radar control, was a bit tricky. Australia had these airports in the boonies. If you were landing at the same time as another plane, that pilot would get on the radio and tell you what he's doing. If somebody on the ground was ready to takeoff, he'd tell you he's holding on the ramp until you landed. The pilots ran the traffic control.

"There was the one time I dropped Billy off on a fishing trip at this small airport in Prescott, Maine. It so happened that day they were having a dedication at the airport because they had re-modeled the terminal.

"The airport was so small there wasn't even much ground to park planes. So when I drop Billy and turn around the jet to leave, the jet exhaust blew all the windows out of the terminal during the dedication ceremony. Of course, we paid for it all.

"There was another time when I was flying Billy from San Diego. We get up in the air and he wants to fix a drink. He goes to get the ice and we had forgotten to put ice in the door. He made us turn around the plane, go back to San Diego, land and pick up ice.

"He could be demanding, but Billy was great to work for. He has always been very generous to me and my family."

Waring Hazelhurst, a retired Dunavant Enterprises buyer in West Tennessee: *"I've known Billy since 1955 or 1956, and we* *were both just starting in the business. He had just graduated from Memphis State and I went to work as a cotton classer for a cotton mill in Bemis, Tennessee, which was owned by the Bemis Brothers Bag Company. Later, I was made an assistant cotton buyer and was made cotton buyer for the mill in Bemis.*

"About half the cotton we bought every year, 50,000 bales, we bought from T.J. White, the company owned by Mr. White and Billy's father Buck. It was also about half the bales they'd sell in a year.

"When Billy's father died, Billy had to make a decision to stay and run his father's company, or accept one of the many job offers he received. Arthur Sharp, who was my boss, encouraged Billy to stay and run the company.

"It didn't surprise me that Billy was successful. I was surprised he got to be the largest cotton merchant in the world. I remember when he made about $35 million in one year on a deal. I said, 'Billy, don't keep gambling your positions.' Of course, he didn't pay me any attention.

"Billy always wanted a position to reverse. One time, he was long on a position when he felt the market changing. He had about 12,000 to 15,000 bales to sell and 8,000 of it was in the Arizona operation run by Clarence Bowe.

"He told Clarence, 'I don't care what you get for the price, I want all the cotton sold by this weekend.'

Monday came and Billy asked Clarence if he had sold the cotton. Clarence said, 'Billy, I tried and I tried, and I could only sell 5,000 bales.'

"Billy says, 'That's all right, I knew you wouldn't get the job done. I sold 5,000 futures for our European operation, so instead of being long at 8,000 we're short at a couple of thousand.'

"About two years after the Bemis company was sold to a Pakistani family, I went to Billy and said, 'I'm not happy. I'd like to go to work for you and represent you in West Tennessee.'

"I worked for him for 27 years. He's generous and fair. He can be very tough since he chewed me out a few times. But that toughness doesn't last. He's got a real soft side.

"Whenever he was down, he never showed it. And he was in place wherever he was. Whether it was on his farm or at the White House, he had a way of fitting in."

"When I got to be 65, I said something about retiring. He said, 'I don't want you to retire.' I got to 70 and I said I wanted to retire. He said, 'I don't want you to retire until I do.'

"Finally, when I was 78, I retired because he sold the company. He called me to apologize about selling, but I said, 'It's time to retire anyway.'

"When I think of Billy, there's nothing but good memories."

Roy Sims, property acquisition for Dunavant Enterprises: *"The reason I stayed with Boss (Billy) so long was, when he told you something you could bank on it. He was about as rough as anybody you'd want to be around. He'd fire you at least once a month. You just slipped back in and he's forgetting about it by then.*

"I went to work for him March 15, 1968. My job was to purchase farms and flip them. The toughest might have been in Kirbyville, South Carolina. I was there almost three years developing that swamp. I said we were going to make a farm out of cypress swamp.

"I almost got myself fired not long after I started working for Boss. He had a black German Shepherd and I had a fine German shepherd female.

"Like an idiot, I got the idea that I'd sure like to have a black German shepherd. So I asked Billy about the chances of my breeding my female with his male. He said, 'Just take my dog with you. When he gets through, bring him back.'

"The second day, Boss' dog is out of the pen and disappeared. This is south of Olive Branch, Mississippi. I looked for that dog

and I thought, 'I've lost the Boss' dog and I don't even know if I got my female bred by him or not. Here he is missing.'

"Late in the afternoon, the Boss' dog comes back. Man, I loaded him up and carried him back to Memphis. I did get a litter of pups and not one of them was black."

Dan Groshens, conservationist, hunting/fishing guide and caretaker of Billy's "Crazy D" ranch outside of Big Timber, Montana: *"Since Billy retired, my job is a lot easier.*

"I've never heard him express regret over anything, wish I would have got that football team or I wish I would have gotten a different ranch.

"I've spent a lot of time with him, especially since he retired and he has never second-guessed himself.

"I asked him, 'Do you ever regret selling your company and retiring?' He said, 'Not a day have I regretted that.' He's pretty comfortable with that.

"Before he retired, it was amazing watching Billy work. In the middle of fishing, he'd answer a satellite phone. Sometimes he'd say, 'I'm playing a fish. I'll call you back.'

And sometimes, we'd stop for an hour while he talked. I'd hear him talk two, three, four hours a day. It was the same business wise. 'What's this? Do that. Do this.'

"He never asked anybody what they thought, he was firing orders out. His mind for numbers was incredible. He'd ask people in his Memphis office, in Wall Street, all over the world, 'What are these numbers?' He already knew them. He just wanted to know if they knew them.

"He used to do the same thing to me. He'd say to me, 'Fishing this part of the stream, where should I throw my fly? Where are the birds going to be?' He already knew the answer. He just wanted me to tell him so I can show him I knew the answer.

"He had zero patience in hunting and fishing when I first started working with him, and that's something that took me a long

time to get used to. The first couple of years were pretty touch-and-go. There were a couple of times I said to my wife, 'I can't do this anymore.' It was pretty rough.

"But since he retired, it's evened out. He sits back and smells the roses a bit more. We've probably become a lot better friends."

Jimmy Wetter, who worked 34 years in Dunavant Enterprises cotton division: *"I started working right out of school in 1976. Though I wanted to be in real estate, he said the cotton business is really growing.*

"He asked me, 'Are you willing to travel? Are you willing to work hard?' I said, 'Yes.' He said, 'I'll put you on a training program and if you do a good job you'll be promoted. When can you start?' I said, 'Anytime'. He said, 'Be here Monday.' And that was it.

"I started working in the sample room in training, then I went into export sales. I lived in Osaka, where the sales office was. I also worked in Fresno and Guatemala City.

"Billy did exactly what he said he'd do. After working in export sales for about 10 years, I was promoted in charge of the Texas/Oklahoma part of the cotton division. I worked there until the business was sold. Billy always took care of me.

"I'd talk to him five to 10 times a day. He wanted to know what was going on in Texas. We'd talk about prices, what we should be buying cotton for, how much we should buy. We'd start the day like that.

"Throughout the day I'd report to Billy. He wanted details and information. He was able to assimilate information without writing it down. He'd know what was going on in the Memphis territory, in California, in all the sales offices. He'd put it all together in his mind and formulate what the market was going to do and how he should structure his position to take advantage of the market.

"When I was in the export sales division, we'd go in every afternoon after the market closed to get offers to send out overseas. Back then it was by Telex. He would remember what prices we offered mills the week before. We were making 30 or 40 offers a night to different textile mills around the world, and he would remember prices. We had them written down, and we'd look back and say, 'He was right. That's what we offered for it.' He never used a calculator. It was all in his mind. He had a real talent for numbers and his memory is awesome.

"His loyalty to us was in return for the loyalty we gave to him. He took care of us. It wasn't just compensation. He'd take us on hunting and fishing trips all over the world. He truly enjoyed being with employees, not a boss-to-employee relationship, but just spending time with them.

"Why leave and work for anybody else when you're working for the best and he's taking care of you? Working for Billy was easy. He'd tell you what to do, he would make decisions quickly and you would just follow through and execute his plan. Ninety percent of the time, he was right."

Kenny Jabbour, who worked in Dunavant Enterprises export sales department: *"I worked under Winfred McGee, head of the export sales department. This would make for a very long days.*

"You'd go up to Mr. Dunavant's office before the market closed, maybe at 3:30 or 4 in the afternoon to discuss the prices you'd put out in the export market that evening. We'd go through every inquiry. It could last 30 minutes or an hour depending how busy we were.

"Mr. Dunavant would just start throwing out numbers for bids. You'd listen with your hands because you're writing so fast. You had to contain a lot of them in your head.

"Mr. Dunavant would jot a couple of things down, but everything else was in his head. There wasn't a bunch of tablets, legal pads and a computer on his desk.

"There was a time where I had to call Mr. Dunavant at 2 a.m. to get a reply about a bid on 16,000 bales of cotton. I didn't want to call him at that time of night, but you also dared not calling him. I call him, he made a decision in 10 seconds and hung up.

"Most of us would have had to get out of bed and grab a calculator. He never got out of bed.

"The next day I said to him, 'Sorry about waking you up.' He said, 'Don't worry about me, I can fall back to sleep.' "

The late Bill Stubblefield, who worked in Dunavant Enterprises: *"We were considering acquiring the McFadden cotton operation and we were deciding how to value it.*

"Billy is sitting at his desk and he just starts writing stuff down. Big letters across this huge white blotter.

"He writes for 30 minutes, rips the paper off the blotter, hands it to us and says, 'That's how I want to buy this company.'

"We all leave his office with this 3-foot by 3-foot piece of paper, sit down and say, 'Okay, let's all figure out what Billy wants in his mind.'

"He had it so sharply in his head as to how he wanted to buy this company, he made these notes that we all had to figure out."

The late Clarence Bowe, Dunavant Enterprises Arizona office: *"From the very first time I met Billy, we hit it off. And once you get to know the man, you know you've got a great friend. That's what life is all about, you know?*

"He was trained by his dad and he fit right in the cotton business. But Billy was a genius. He had the ability to trade with people all over the world and he'd trade a guy out of his britches before the guy knew it.

"All you had to do with Billy was give him information. He never wanted to hear anybody talking a lot. He'd just want the information.

"You'd tell him, 'This guy in Arizona wants to sell us 10,000 bales of cotton.' He'll tell you right then to buy it or not buy it. I don't think it ever took him more than two minutes to make up his mind about a deal.

"Just about every decision Billy made was correct, which is why he was so successful. And when it wasn't the right decision, it didn't bother him. The average guy would worry about it, but Billy didn't worry about nothing. That's just about impossible to do. Most people start worrying about making a deal as soon as they start playing with it.

"Billy brought me and a lot of other people on fishing and hunting trips all over the world. Every year, we would go someplace different and every trip was fun. He made it that way.

"There was that hunting trip to Cuba where armed guards searched our car and found all of our ammunition. That was scary at that moment, but we were all young, so we usually weren't too scared of anything.

"There was another trip we took where I set up a lot of the arrangements, and nothing went right. Billy fired me a bunch of times on that trip, but if you worked for Billy you got used to being fired. You never took that stuff seriously.

"I love and adore the man. Billy is the most remarkable person I've ever met."

Wesley Ross, who co-manages Billy's Quail Hollow farm in Coffeeville, Mississippi: *"I've worked for Mr. Billy 18 years. I just came to the farm one day to work the combine and I've been working for him ever since.*

"He's easy to work for. He just wants what he wants. If he tells you something, that's what he wants. He's dead serious every time he talks to you."

Luke Purdy, who co-manages Billy's Quail Hollow farm in Coffeeville, Mississippi: *"I knew Mr. Billy before I started working for him five years ago. My Dad owned Quail Hollow and sold it to Mr. Billy.*

"I hadn't any problem working for him. You have no problem with him if you do what he asks of you.

"He's never gotten mad with me. He probably knows who to get mad with and who not to. He tells you when you do a good job. And if you don't, he'll let you know that, also.

"He's a fair man, a man of his word. He does what he says he's going to do. If you need something to do your job, he makes sure you get it."

John T. Gaston, who manages Billy's Mallard Rest farm in Webb, Mississippi: *"I've worked for Mr. Billy for 28 years. He can be hard to work for at times, but he's also he's a good man. I've been hunting with him a few times. He's the best shot I've ever seen. Nobody shoots ducks like he does. He likes to shoot (a lot of shots). He's fair and he's funny with just everybody. He's always liked me and he's made that clear to everybody on the farm. I'm* *loyal to him because he has been loyal to me. He's 100 percent a man of his word. I love him."*

Greg Thompson, security guard at the Dunavant home in Memphis: *"Mr. D taught me respect. The first time I met him he called me 'sir.' From then on, I respected everybody. I have been working for Mr. D for 25 years, and he has never disrespected me as an employee or a man."*

Sidney Shields, Dunavant Enterprises mailroom head clerk and courier: *"I've been with Billy 14 years. My relationship with him is different than anybody else in the office. I know him as a person, not a businessman. A lot of people can be intimidated by him because he can be intimidating at times. All he wants you to do is do your job, no excuses. If you don't know the answer, find the answer. He says what he means and he means what he says.*

"If he gets mad at you, it doesn't linger. He can bite into you at 10:30 and at 10:40 when you walk back in his office it's over. He's consistent, he's firm, he's fair and he's a giver."

The Chickasaw Council appreciated Billy's lifelong support of the Boy Scouts. In 1983, his fundraising exceeded their goal by more than a half-million dollars.

13

You Can't Take It With You

I LOVE GIVING MONEY, BUT I HAVE NOT ALWAYS BEEN a giver.

All that changed one day when I went to visit Abe Plough.

Mr. Plough was a brilliant businessman who built Schering-Plough, a pharmaceutical and consumer product manufacturer that has produced products familiar to all of us, such as St. Joseph children's aspirin, Maybelline cosmetics and Dr. Scholl's foot powder.

I was in my late 20s raising money for the Boy Scouts of America, so I went to call on Mr. Plough, who must have been almost 80 years old back then. He was a friend and someone I tremendously respected, so when he said "Jump," I jumped.

He called me "Boy" because I was one. I entered his office and he said, "Boy, come in. What do you want from me?" I said, "Mr. Plough, I want you to give some money to the Boy Scouts.'

Now as chairman of the campaign, I had committed $5,000 and I thought that was plenty. But Mr. Plough looked at me and said, "Boy, your campaign is going to fall right on its ass. It ain't going nowhere if you're not the lead giver."

I've never forgotten that. I got the message early that if you're going to ask for money, you've got to play it as well as they are going to play it.

So I ended up pledging $100,000 to the Boy Scouts. What Mr. Plough said always drove me to be the lead giver of things I always raised money for.

I really do love giving, so much so that I never get tired of it. Once I became a giver, it changed my life. It gives me a great zest.

I've donated to schools, churches, libraries, the arts, conservation, even zoos. I donated some money to the Memphis Zoo and told Tommie I bought some monkeys in her honor.

Some men give their true love diamonds. I buy monkeys in Tommie's honor. Nothing says "I love you" like monkeys.

I relate to a quote that has been attributed to British Prime Minister Winston Churchill who supposedly said, "We make a living by what we get, but we make a life by what we give."

Tommie worries about me getting so many donation requests:

"I said to Billy one time, 'Don't you get tired every week of having a stack of letters on your desk from people asking for money? How do you decide where to give?'

"He replied, 'It's up to me to sort through it, pray about what I'm supposed to give. I never resent anybody asking me. It doesn't mean I'm going to give to everybody. It's just a calling of my life. People know I have money. I'm blessed to be a blessing, but not to everybody.'

"Often times, he'll get a repeat donation request. I said, 'You gave them $50,000 last year, and they are coming around again.' He said, 'Well, they got it the first time and they might get it the second time.'

"Billy understands that God has blessed him to be a blessing to others. He's always felt wherever he's planted, whether it's in Memphis or the farm in Mississippi or the ranches in Montana and Texas, he's going to support that community.

"In Melville, the tiny town near our Montana ranch, he paid for the town's fire truck and to construct a school. He built tennis courts in Big Timber because he found out the wife of Dan Gros-

hens, our Montana ranch conservationist, likes to play tennis and the town had no courts.

"In Texas, he gave $5,000 to an injured veteran he didn't even know.

"Often times, Billy will give money and immediately forget that he did. When he does it, the curtain comes down and it's done. He doesn't need a pat on the back or a plaque hung in his honor. There are no strings attached when he gives.

"He just loves to give. We'll be walking sometimes and he'll say something like, 'Remind me to send $10,000 to The Neighborhood School (which is actually the name of the school he helped build).' One of the reasons I fell in love with him is I've never known somebody with such a giving heart.

"I once asked Billy, 'How much money have you given away in your lifetime?' He said, 'I don't know, I have no idea.' So I started researching it and discovered he'd given away more than $40 million.

"That was two decades ago."

I weigh the donation requests I receive and measure how much I will give. It's really pretty easy. I find it interesting that some people with beaucoups of money just don't want to give. That's okay.

I still make money every year, even though I'm retired from the cotton business. I had to start giving away money. What else was I going to do with it? I've given my children plenty, and they're all grown.

I used to love to make money, but I heard all my life there's joy in giving. Let me tell you, it's true. I have enjoyed giving it away to some of the following people and organizations for various reasons:

Trow Gillespie, co-founder and president of NewSouth Capital Management Corp. in Memphis: *"Billy has helped* *me out in fundraising in so many ways. I was chairing the Memphis University School campaign, and one of our first calls was to Billy. It was about the fifth time I called on him for something.*

"We walked in the room and said, 'Billy, we really need your help on this. You'll set the tone for the whole campaign.' He said, 'All right, I'm going to do this. But if I ever see you in this office again, I'll have the guard remove you.'

"I think he was joking. But I never went back to his office again asking for money.

"Father Don Mowery, who used to run Youth Services, was working on a fundraising campaign with me that Billy was chairing. He said, 'I'm going to tell you one thing about Billy Dunavant. He is the only person I've ever known who has completely figured out the joy of giving. Everything he gives, he relishes.'

"Billy loves giving. His generosity is amazing."

Dr. Shirley Raines, former University of Memphis president: *"I grew up on a farm in West Tennessee that grew cotton and my Dad and later my brother sold their cotton to Billy's company. So I had a connection with him when I met him for the first time after I became the University of Memphis president in 2001.*

"I went to meet him with Willard Sparks, one of Billy's friends. Billy said at the end of our first meeting, 'I like you, Madam President. I think you'll be all right.'

"It didn't take long before I learned how involved Billy was in the community and how proud he was to be a U of M alum.

"Billy also became a good friend of John Calipari, our basketball coach. I know Billy let John use his jet at times to recruit.

"One day, I get a call from Billy and he says, 'You need to make sure you take care of John, we've got to keep him here.' Of course, I could feel John's fingerprints all over that phone call. But Billy wasn't afraid to speak up for people he believed in.

"Any friend of Willard Sparks, whose judgment I trusted, was a friend of mine. For Willard to take me to meet Billy early on

Billy and Peggy Wellford dedicate the Dunavant-Wellford Tennis Center at Memphis University School.

was quite an endorsement. And through the years, Billy's wife Tommie often sent me notes of encouragement, which I certainly appreciated."

Bill Morris, former Shelby County mayor who worked with Billy to relocate Ducks Unlimited to Memphis: *"Getting Ducks Unlimited to relocate in Memphis from Chicago was a major coup for us because it's worldwide. It has a membership of more than 500,000 and they are the finest environmentalists on earth.*

"I wanted them to come to Memphis because they are a prestigious organization. Secondly, I wanted to protect the 500-year water we have underneath this city and get them to maintain and monitor the water quality.

"Billy was the reason we started looking at Ducks Unlimited. He stayed the course, and he put his money where his mouth was. He gave at least $1 million. We matched it with the taxpayers' money and we made it happen.

"It was a partnership, and that's what happens when people like Billy Dunavant get involved. If government would listen and participate in those things attractive to a city, we'd do a lot more of that.

"We had a lot of competition to get Ducks Unlimited. We had a prime location at Shelby Farms where we could give them a multimillion-dollar property. Billy had the muscle to talk to everybody in the organization to really push this thing.

"Ever since he was a young executive, Billy has been a player in those initiatives that say, 'We're going to make our community better.'

"He was the same with the Boy Scouts. He had a genuine understanding of the Boy Scout oath. He put up all the money for the Chickasaw Council headquarters. I was president for three years and Billy was at every event we did.

"When we started the Ambassador organization at the University of Memphis, Fred Smith of FedEx and I were named co-chairs to raise the money. We came up with the idea that $500,000 gets you a place at the table for whatever happens at the U of M ad infinitum.

"We put together this presentation with all these drawings of expansion and buildings. I went to school with Billy, so I decide to take U of M President Lane Rawlins and athletic director R.C. Johnson with me to Billy's office to make a presentation. Lane didn't know Billy.

"We get to Billy's office and sit down. I started showing all these posters in our demonstration.

"Billy said, 'Just tell me what you want. I'm not going to look at the goddamned posters.'

"I said, 'Shit, yes you are. We put in a lot of work to put these goddamned posters together.'

"He said, 'I'm going to do the deal. Don't put those goddamned posters up.'

"I said, 'Billy, we went to a lot of trouble. By God, you're going to look at these posters.'

"Lane Rawlins is sitting there on the side and I thought he was going to have a heart attack. He didn't know my relationship with Billy.

"Finally we showed the posters and Billy put in the $500,000.

"Billy knows enough about what you're doing. If the plan is out there and it makes sense, he's a player.

"You don't bullshit Billy. You really don't, because he has been there and back long before you got to the damned table.

"I've had so much appreciation for Billy. He is apolitical, in the sense that politics don't interest him if you're not a good guy. If he likes you, he'll stay with you. He doesn't like the bullshit politics, even though in his business he has to have a direct line to the political system.

"He took on a yeoman's job. He took risks and built a megalopolis organization that went into different areas worldwide.

"I'm an admirer for all Billy Dunavant stands for. He's one of the most sensitive, emotional guys I've ever met. On many occasions, I've been in his presence when he has been honored for doing good things. The tears would flow unabashedly. That says a lot about a guy. A real man can cry. He has a strong, deep inward faith."

Dale Hall, Ducks Unlimited chief executive officer: *"It's hard to put a value on what Billy has done for us, because he has done it in so many different ways. It's not only his philanthropy, but also his getting others to be philanthropists and conservationists.*

Billy was key in bringing Ducks Unlimited to Memphis. The portrait of Billy and his dog, Bully, hangs in the front entryway of the group's headquarters at the Agricenter.

"Once he decides the cause is worthy, he will do everything he can to help. Having Billy Dunavant in is a phenomenal asset when you're trying to get anything done.

"He and Tommie are tenacious conservationists, and they are tenacious citizens. My first week on the job here five years ago, they walked in the door and told me, 'If there is anything we can do to help, let us know.' They've been with us the whole way. They are wonderful, wonderful people.

"Billy analyzes things faster than any person I've ever met. He'll ask you questions, 'What did you mean here? And here? And here?' Once he gets those answers, he can assimilate the facts and the situation becomes clear as a bell to him.

"Our mission is conservation, putting wetlands and grasslands back on the landscape, and Billy loves that. If there is anything I've ever asked him for, I've never heard 'no.' Never.

"But I am respectful and I don't ask for something unless it's important. Now he will get up each time and say, 'This is the last time I'm doing this.' And then he does it again the next year.

"Billy is an icon that will never be matched in Memphis as far as his wide scope of influence."

Susan Schadt, former president/CEO of ArtsMemphis and co-creator of Conservation Through Art: *"In 2005, the U.S. Fish and Wildlife Service approached Ducks Unlimited about moving the federal duck stamp contest out of Washington, D.C., for the first time in 72 years. Due to the magnitude of this national art competition of original art, Ducks Unlimited requested involvement from ArtsMemphis, our city's 50-year-old arts fund.*

"While we were eager to help, the collaboration wasn't a natural one. Ducks Unlimited, a massive national non-profit fundraising machine and the world's leader in wetlands and waterfowl conservation. By comparison, we were a smallish arts fund in Memphis with a staff of eight people. And, what would our leadership think of arts and ducks?

"I didn't know if this proposal was the right one to take on. But Andy Dolich, president of the Grizzlies at the time, who was on the ArtsMemphis board, convinced me that in Memphis if an idea involved hunters, I needed to get back to Ducks Unlimited with a resounding 'yes.'

"Now we had to develop a plan. We needed a team. Serendipitously, that very day I was invited to fish with John Stokes. Perfect. It was in that boat that the idea was spawned. The first hook was creating this initiative by memorializing Harry Phillips, respected businessman and philanthropist, beloved by multitudes and especially by John and Billy Dunavant, who had been searching for a way to pay tribute to him. John called Billy and within a matter of days, we had the 'SWAT' team in place.

"And it worked. It has been brilliant. Billy, along with Tommie, has been our chair four times and our honoree in 2006. He has raised money for us over six events encompassing nine years. He created our legacy.

"When we first approached Billy about becoming involved, he said, 'I'm not that artsy.' I said, 'I know you're not, but you've got some of the finest sporting life art and sculptures and carvings in the world. The oldest documentation of wildlife is through art and of course, Ducks Unlimited is here because of you. Help us with this partnership.' We came up with the name 'Conservation Through Art.'

"Through 2014, we have raised $4.4 million for the two organizations through this program. And 72 percent of those donations were from people who had certainly contributed to conservation efforts but never before given donations to ArtsMemphis.

"We created a week-long series of events around the event that first year in 2005 and we raised $650,000. It was so successful, the U.S. Fish and Wildlife Service wanted to come back to Memphis in 2006.

"So in 2006, we had two weeks worth of events, we honored Billy and we raised $985,000. We sent out invitations to people all over the country. Amazing results came from those that wanted to pay tribute to Billy. One day we opened one of our Conservation Through Art return envelopes and a $10,000 check fell out from a California friend and colleague of Billy's.

"We had just finished '06 when Billy called me to meet with him. We did this after every event, a debrief. Always probing, how much did we raise, net proceeds and what would we do differently. We went through all that, and then he got quiet and focused.

"He said, 'Now I'm going to tell you something you're not going to like. It is my suggestion to redshirt this initiative for next year. This pace is going to wear out our donors. It might be smart of us to take something that's really working and not have it

until '08. You don't have to answer me right now. I know you're disappointed.'

"And what he said next was important and typically Billy. He told me to think about it. That this was my decision. He said, 'I feel strongly about this redshirting and Tommie and I will Chair the event again for one more year, whatever your decision, after that, we're done. That's it.' (They continued chairing in 2008, 2010 and 2014).

"I went to my car, called 'a friend' to discuss Billy's idea. Then I thought about it. If the smartest businessman and the best fund-raiser I've ever had on my team is telling me we should redshirt the event, I probably should listen.

"I called him from the Dunavant Enterprises parking lot and said, 'Billy, I didn't know what I was thinking. I should have said yes right away.' He told me he knew me better than that, but 'thanks for making the right decision.'

"That's when we started every other year and it really set in place the legacy of the initiative.

"In '08, we didn't have the U.S. Fish and Wildlife Service involved, so no art contest. Ducks Unlimited had the conservation part covered but we still needed an appropriate arts focus. I decided on a 'shoot for the moon' opportunity and asked Billy and John Stokes how they would feel if their private hunting lodges were photographed and displayed publicly.

"They agreed and enlisted other hunters to agree to have their lodges and clubs photographed. I've never seen an idea come to fruition so fast. These guys get things done.

"It immediately gave me the idea to follow up the photography with a book and that's when we started our book series.

"Billy was always quick to make a decision and execute. One day, we were having a steering committee meeting at Chuck Smith's house to discuss '06 plans. Chuck has been on our steering committee for five events and is a very close friend of Billy's.

I knew Paul Tudor Jones, Billy's cousin, had one of the world's most important collections of duck decoys.

"So I asked Billy if he thought Paul would allow us to showcase the decoys in our Memphis Brooks Museum, which would involve transporting, curating, promoting and a multitude of commitment and details.

"Billy gets up from the table, picks up the phone, calls Paul, hangs up and says, 'It's done. What's next on your list?' Paul sent his entire decoy collection to Memphis with his curator, set it up at the Brooks and he came for the opening of the exhibit.

"It was amazing to see Billy work like that. He is an unbelievable fundraiser. When he says he's going to make his calls, he makes his calls. But he'd also tell our committee members, 'Why haven't you made these calls? You need to make these calls.'

"Chuck Smith once told us that when Billy is in the fundraising mode or wants to get something done, the five most feared words you could hear are 'Billy Dunavant's on the phone.'

Buck Dunavant, one of Billy's sons: *"When I look at everything my Dad has done, one of the best things he ever did was bringing the Ducks Unlimited headquarters to Memphis.*

"If you look at the new Bass Pro Shop in The Pyramid which has the Ducks Unlimited Waterfowl Heritage Center, it wouldn't be in Memphis if it wasn't for Dad.

"I know Dad owned the Showboats and brought pro tennis to Memphis, but getting Ducks Unlimited to move to Memphis is one of the greatest gifts he's ever given the city. Not only has it brought jobs to the city, but it also put Memphis in the map in a lot of different ways.

"It makes me proud that one of Dad's earlier deeds is still reaping rewards for the city of Memphis."

Tim Finchem, commissioner of the PGA tour: *"Billy had acquired 6,500 acres of property in the 1970s in St. Augustine.*

Deane Beman, my predecessor and some of our staff met with Billy about risking his property for the development of a World Golf Hall of Fame.

"Billy had acquired the property down there that butts up against the interstate in St. Augustine. After meeting with Deane, Billy jumped in 100 percent and helped move the process of developing a broader vision.

"It wasn't just the Hall of Fame. It was two golf courses and it became an area that had a lot of different uses. That was important to making it happen, because Halls of Fame don't make money, they are subsidized. This one was assisted with licensing fees of the various retail operations. We put PGA Tour production down there.

"Then years later, Billy was an initial trustee of the First Tee program and he helped us get it going (by donating $1 million). He looked at it, and he saw the possibilities of that program taking off in 10,000 public schools reaching millions of kids in every state.

"He has been a great friend of the PGA tour and I appreciate him because he is an old-school guy. Lawyers are an afterthought when he makes a deal with you. When he gives you a handshake, looks you in the eye and says, 'Let's do this,' you know it's going to happen."

Father Don Mowery, founder of Youth Service Memphis and Youth Service USA: *"Billy's the most generous person I've ever known. There are people who can afford to give who won't give you a dime. Billy will give you the shirt off his back if he believes in you.*

"I started a program to keep inner-city kids occupied. Since we had no big place to do this, I appealed to the Navy base in Millington. I asked if we could use some of their facilities and have a program for kids in the summer. I was originally turned down, but they changed their minds.

"One day my board president was with the Cotton Council. He said to me, 'I want to bring Billy Dunavant over here.' Billy came to one of our graduations at St. Mary's Cathedral. He was so impressed that he stayed afterward and said he wanted to get involved.

"About that time we were getting ready to have a capital funds campaign and we were looking for somebody to head it up. Somebody suggested Billy, so we made an appointment to see him.

"We asked him if he'd head the campaign. He said, 'I'd be honored. And I guarantee you one thing. It will be successful.' That's what I wanted to hear.

"We'd meet with Billy in his office and go over names and corporations we needed to call on. Billy took at least half of them. There were some people that none of us knew, including Billy, but he'd say, 'I'm going to sure get to know them.'

"Within a couple of weeks, he had all his calls made. Everybody else was way behind, but Billy was leading the pack.

"He was that way in every single thing I dealt with him on. He said, 'Yes' or 'No', and if he said 'Yes' you knew it would be a done deal and be done in the time frame he said.

"From our program in Millington, thanks to Billy's influence and people knowing him, we began one in Blytheville, Arkansas. That was successful.

"We went to Barksdale Air Force in Shreveport, Louisiana. We met with General David Jones, who became the chairman of the Joint Chiefs of Staff. General Jones said, 'I'd like to have one of these programs on every one of my Air Force bases.'

"We had Navy, Air Force and then General Westmoreland with the Army got involved, so we had all three branches of the service. We got it all blessed by the Department of Defense, which asked us if we'd consider doing the program all over the United States.

"By this time, we were running by the seat of our pants. That's when we organized it nationally. We have two programs – Youth

Billy with Father Don Mowery and Phil Burnett, president of the Youth Service Board, after a Youth Service graduation at St. Mary's Cathedral.

Service Memphis, which we started here, and Youth Service USA that expanded to include 125 bases all over the country.

"As busy as Billy was, I could make a telephone call to Shirley his secretary or to him or to Tommie, and I got an answer right away. They were very much interested in what we were doing. Tommie became interested. She's something else, I guarantee you.

"With the money that Billy raised in our capital campaign, we were able to expand our program and start other new programs like Bridges.

"Having Billy's name on the board list always helped because so many people knew him and knew of his generosity. Then we began to go to the private sector, and that's how we began to raise considerably more money than just the capital funds campaign.

"I think it's hard for people to say no because they knew Billy wouldn't be involved in anything that wasn't a good program. Billy's name was a stamp of approval and they knew Billy would

not put up with any tomfoolery. If he had his name on it, he believed in it."

Ellis Haguewood, Headmaster of Memphis University School: *"A great school can't be truly great without great supporters. Billy has been just amazing.*

"He and his family have been invested in MUS for a lifetime. Five sons attended MUS and four of them graduated from here. He's had four grandsons graduate and three more are current students.

"I don't know where we'd be without Billy. There's no way to quantify what his philanthropic support has meant to us. He has been wonderfully generous, contributing to everything from our capital projects to our endowments to our annual fund.

"He only has told me no once, and he didn't mean it.

"And he just didn't contribute his money. He gave us his time. He was on our Board of Trustees from 1967 to 1982 and after that moved to our honorary board. He has long-range vision and contributed ideas from the very beginning of MUS.

"Billy first contributed in the 1980s to our endowment campaign to support MUS faculty, and then was a big contributor to the Sue H. Hyde Sports and Physical Education Center.

"He funded the original Wellford tennis courts that were built in 1977 and then made a lead gift to build our new 12-court Dunavant-Wellford Tennis Center. Then he gifted the lower school when we built that, and there's a lecture hall named in honor of his parents that we call the Dunavant Lecture Hall.

"He gave a lead gift, including a large contribution plus a request in our 'Doors to New Opportunities' campaign that re-invented our facilities in the late 1990s and early 2000s.

"The entire upper school building is named in his honor. It's called the Dunavant Upper School and there's a great portrait of him in this building done by the late Marshall Bouldin III, his favorite portrait artist.

"His support of MUS, in a sense, was part of his long-range vision for his business and enterprises. But he also has the same long-range vision for education.

"He's in an elite category of people who understand the real value of building not just Memphis, but the world, through education.

"It's not just the academic area Billy is interested in. It's character, it's leadership, opportunities for the boys to learn how to serve and lead. He understands that has to happen early in the life of a boy if that boy is going to contribute leadership when he's a man.

"Billy is a very strong Christian, and he and I have talked about Christianity at MUS. The new MUS is an extension of the old Presbyterian Day School back in the day.

"He is one of the great philanthropists of all-time in Memphis. If you added up all the gifts he's made to non-profit organizations, it would be phenomenal. He's a great man and role model for our boys."

John Dobbs Sr., owner of Dobbs Management Services based in Memphis: *"Billy hasn't asked me to do much, but when he does ask I do it. He got me to give the largest donation I've given to anybody. He called me up, asked for it and I said 'Yes' on the spot. I didn't even think about it. Because he's always done things to help me, I try to figure ways to return the favors."*

Greg Duckett, senior vice-president and corporate counsel for the Baptist Memorial Health Care system in Memphis: *"I was president of the AutoZone Liberty Bowl in 2001, and I can say if it wasn't for his involvement in the Liberty Bowl, we probably wouldn't still have the Liberty Bowl. He stepped up and John Q. Public still doesn't know the role he played. He stabilized and turned that bowl around financially. He understood the importance of the event.*

"Billy is a down-to-earth person who has a heart as big as the city of Memphis itself."

Kelli Dunavant, Billy and Tommie's daughter: *"I grew up in a loving environment with parents who cared for the world and the people around them. God gave me a charitable heart from birth and even the simplest of injustices would wreck me.*

"I saw things that hurt me, but I didn't know how to change them. Dad showed me what it means to give and be a world changer and it's not necessarily about money.

"Dad's lesson is about using what's in your hand. Sometimes, it's money and sometimes it's service. Dad served people who needed serving, he employed people who needed employment and he showered those people with love.

"He never asked people to give money to a cause he had not contributed to himself. In 2 Corinthians 9:7, it says, 'Each of you should give what you have decided in your heart to give, not reluctantly and not under compulsion. For God loves a cheerful giver.'

"If there is anybody who embodies that scripture, it is my father. I've never known a more cheerful giver. He gives from his heart, he gives joyfully and not out of compulsion. The torch was passed to me and it still lights my path. The older I get, the more I use his wisdom and embody his strength."

Money doesn't solve everything, but it can make things move in the right direction.

I'm not finished giving yet and I'll be giving when I've left this life. I have a foundation that will continue to help many organizations, particularly focusing on youth groups and conservation.

Jesus changed how I lived my life and how I gave. I gave my heart, when I felt God said to give. There's a real joy that comes from giving. It makes me smile. Who needs credit when giving makes you feel that good? Giving is contagious.

Tommie and Billy at their home in East Memphis

14

Tommmmmmmiiiiieeeeee

I DON'T THINK AFTER TWO MARRIAGES THAT I WAS looking to get married again. But what struck me on my first date with Tommie was how easy it was to communicate with her. She says she had some preconceived notions about me:

"My image of Billy before we went out was that he's a very wealthy man, he wanted a sexy girl to travel with, that he was very materialistic. People who don't get the opportunity to meet Billy wouldn't believe what a humble, down-to-earth, loving caring person he is.

"I never met anybody with such a heart. You could just feel Billy's heart. I never met anybody that gave like he did and does. I never met anybody that was such a giver, that cared about people, that was truly concerned, that gave to his friends. He cared about everybody who worked for him."

Tommie and I entered the relationship from different places. I was a divorcé and she was a widow, but she remembers how we got together:

"I didn't meet Billy until about three years after my husband died and I moved back to Memphis after living in England where I'd gone to school at Oxford.

"The different perspective for me was I came from death. I didn't get a divorce. My husband died suddenly in a tragic car accident, so I knew the value of having love again. I always thought

I'd re-marry because I always thought I'd be a better wife because I knew life could change in 9 to 5. I talked to my husband Earl at 9 o'clock in the morning when I left to go to work and I was coming in from work when the phone rang with the news he had died. Your life can change in one workday.

"I met Billy through a mutual friend. One day Ann Marie Dobbs said, 'You need to meet Billy Dunavant.' I said, 'I'm not interested in anybody.' But she thought I was exactly what Billy needed in his life to make him a happy man. Because I was organized and structured, I was already like him. He was fast-paced and moving and so am I.

"Ann Marie thought I was what Billy needed and he was what I needed, which was stability after grief and someone older to help with my financial stuff I inherited when my husband died.

"She took me to the tennis tournament. She said, 'He's right up there, let's go meet him.' Finally I said, 'Ann Marie, you arrange the date. I will go out with him and he will see that I'm not anything he wants. I want marriage. I'm a strong Christian. These are my values. I won't be what he wants. I'm not a sexy girl. I'm just going to go to dinner.' "

As it turned out, Tommie is exactly who I wanted and needed. I think our first two dates impressed her. At the very least, they were entertaining.

"Ann Marie arranges a dinner date for me to go to Justine's with Billy. He arrives to pick me up. I go out to get in the car and it smells unbelievably bad, like something is rotten. Billy has no sense of smell, so he doesn't smell it.

"I said, 'Billy, there's something dead in your car. We're going to have to take my car.' Later we found out that the kids had left real Easter eggs in the trunk of his car for about three weeks. He had to get rid of the car.

"Once we got to Justine's, I spent the whole time telling him who I am, what my thoughts and values were, what I'd been through, what I wanted in life. After that we went to the Belmont.

"John Dunavant, one of Billy's sons, later said to me, 'I knew my father had really found something special by his voice the next day when we were going turkey hunting in Texas and he took great pride that we were staying in a tacky-ass trailer with no telephone. That morning, he was on the phone yelling at David Belew about getting a phone in that trailer. He had to have a phone. I said, 'Dad, why did you have to have a phone? It's the weekend, we're not trading.' He said, 'I've got to call Tommie.' I knew by his voice there was something different about it. It was different than my Mom, and it was different from Ann (Billy's second wife). There was something different.'

"On our second date, Billy took me to the movie Pretty Woman, *where Richard Gere takes Julia Roberts on an airplane and to the opera.*

"The next night after our second date, Billy says 'I'm going to pick you up and we're going to dinner.' So he picks me up, takes me to the airport, his plane is waiting and he takes me to New Orleans for dinner.

"We started dating."

When we first started dating, Tommie didn't know anything about the outdoors. All she did was jog and study and do ballet, but she fell into the outdoor things beautifully. That was amazing, but she recalls welcoming my outdoor life:

"Billy was about the outdoors, and I hadn't been. But I found coming from grief, I liked being outdoors. Even before I met Billy when I was in England after Earl died, I liked being outside. There was something about being outside that brought life to me. I loved to take Kelli and go to the park. I just felt like I had to

Tommie and Billy relaxing at their ranch in Montana.
PHOTOGRAPH BY KAREN PULFER FOCHT / *THE COMMERCIAL APPEAL* / LANDOV

be out. I felt I was suffocating inside. I was walking through the journey of grief.

"I loved the fact Billy was about the outside. I just took to everything he did outside – hunting and fishing. The trips we took and the places we have traveled as a result of his hunting and fishing. I have seen the world.

"I'm not a selfish person. I go with the flow. Whatever the agenda is, I'm happy with it. I love to cook and entertain. I never liked the country club social scene. That's for people who like to do that, and that's great. But I don't like to dress up and do all that. I'm just happy at home being comfortable and cooking something."

It has been easy for me because Tommie has been a giver since the day she said hello. She never thinks of herself. She

Billy and Tommie at the night of the open house for the new Dunavant headquarters on Ridgeway in East Memphis.

"I said, 'That's okay.' I said, 'What's the dress? He said, 'Oh, it's just casual. I'm just going down to Mississippi to give a speech.'

"So I thought, 'We're going to Mississippi, it's in the fall, maybe I'd wear something like you'd wear to an Ole Miss football game.' So I had this cute little pants outfit on with this scarf.

"When we walk in, there's a few people under 70 and all these women were dressed in velvet and rhinestone dresses.

"Billy is fine because he's wearing a dark suit and tie. I'm trying my best to be invisible, so I went and sat down. I look at him and he knows he's in trouble. He knows this is one of the things I really stress about. I was very obviously underdressed and having to sit at the head table.

"So he thought a way to explain my dress was to go around and tell people I had hemorrhoids. How he thought of this, I will never know.

He'd tell them, 'Bless her heart, she's such a good sport, she wanted to be here with me, she didn't feel like getting dressed but she came anyway.'

"Soon, all these older women one-by-one would come over and say, 'Awwww honey, puttin' on those 'ol pantyhose is hard when you got them 'rhoids.'

"I didn't know what they were taking about. I'd never had hemorrhoids and never had a discussion about hemorrhoids. Finally someone told me, 'We know how hard it was for you to come here today with hemorrhoids.'

"Billy could have told them I had a stomach ache or something. But hemorrhoids? We'd been married just three or four months when that happened."

You have to have a sense of humor to tolerate me, and thankfully Tommie did. She never knew when I might pull a prank on her, like the time we went turkey hunting along a canal in Florida.

Right before I quietly move to sneak a shot at a turkey, I tell Tommie to lie on the ground flat and not make a sound. She's never forgotten what happened next:

"I'm on the ground because Billy told me to get there and not to spook the turkey. All of a sudden, I feel something crawling all over me and pulling my hair.

"I take a peek and I'm surrounded on all sides by what I found out later are baby otters. I knew if I moved and spooked the turkey I'd be in trouble, but I also knew if I stayed on the ground being gnawed on by these creatures I would die.

"Thankfully, the turkey left and Billy came back."

Sometimes, I just can't help myself when a situation presents itself that I can string Tommie along. She recalls the occasion when we checked into a motel in Ennis, Montana:

"We pulled into our motel and Billy got out to check in. The kids were already planning their evening swim in the outdoor pool, and I was ready to settle in our room.

"Billy came back from the registration cabin with a concerned look on his face, and he stated, 'Well, there's been a little mix-up.' I pressed him further. He told me the hotel had double-booked our room by accident, and we would have to be forced to share a room.

"I was appalled at the thought, but he kept going, 'Oh it should be fine. Bob and Leticia are very nice people, and they'll have one bed and we'll have the other. No problems.'

"I was adamant that I was not inclined to share a tiny motel room with a couple we had never met before. The more I fussed, the more he assured me Bob and Leticia would be great, and that we should just go on in and meet them. He opens the door, gingerly calling out for Bob and Leticia. 'Bob? Leticia? It's Billy and Tommie. Bob?'

"I'm behind him trying to calm myself, but my head is screaming, 'This is ridiculous!' In the room, the bathroom door is closed, and the light is on. Billy tells me that Bob must be taking a shower, and we'll wait for him to get out. We're standing in a motel room waiting for a man we don't know to get out of the shower!

"In the end, there turned out to be no Bob and Leticia, but Billy really had me going for a good 30 minutes or more. He's always been great at creating a full story and getting a rise out of me."

Taking care of me can be a full-time job, especially when we're on a trip like the one we had to Scotland, when we happened to have a flat tire while driving. I guess it was my fault, as Tommie remembers:

"We rented a car and Billy insisted on driving. Driving on the opposite side of the road proved to be more of a challenge than he thought. He got too close to curbs, fences and even bumped a cow.

"The cow didn't flinch, but Billy's demolition derby finished with a flat tire. We got out of the car to change it. I pulled out all the tools and instructions. As I'm working to get things together, I'm chatting with him.

"I remove the flat and I go ask a question about the next step. Billy isn't standing there. I get up to look and my husband is fishing!

"He retrieved his rod from the car, left me to change the tire and he's walking up and down the stream fishing.

"I could have used a mimosa at that point."

Among the many things Tommie and I share in common is our love of dogs.

We've had nine dogs and let me see if I can name them all – Simba, Tomasina, Chief, Bully Dog, Montana, Sadie, Pippie, Sampson and Atom Cat.

Along with our granddog Mr. Bean, these dogs have been our heart.

Montana was probably my favorite dog of all-time, and not just because he took a bite out of John Stokes Sr. the first time I invited him hunting.

Montana was a German shepherd that I trained to retrieve ducks. Tommie will vouch for this:

"We took Montana hunting as a puppy with Bully Dog and he'd watch Bully Dog retrieve. All of a sudden one day, he just jumped out of the blind and brought back a crippled duck. Montana was amazing. He went salmon fishing with Billy in Canada. He went fly fishing with Billy in Montana. Montana went everywhere we went. I don't think I've ever loved a dog like I loved Montana."

Chief was a dog that used to ride with Tommie every morning when she took our daughter Kelli to school at Hutchison. Tommie says they had a daily routine that Chief loved:

"I'd drop Kelli at school and then I'd take Chiefy through the McDonald's drive-through line because he loved Egg McMuffins. Chiefy would sit in the back seat, I'd roll down the window and they would give Chiefy his Egg McMuffin.

"When Chiefy died, I called the McDonalds we always drove through, told them Chiefy had died and he wouldn't be coming for his Egg McMuffin.

"They sent me flowers."

Tommie named our two current dogs, Simba and Tomasina. Why? She explains:

"We've named our dogs together, but sometimes Billy or I will come up with a name. I named Simba right after we returned from Africa where we followed a pride of lions.

"When we got home, our housesitter had just gone and picked up this new dog for us.

"This dog had the longest whiskers and his feet looked like lion paws. I said, 'He's Simba, he's the Lion King.' It looked like I arrived home to my own little cub. He was a chubby little thing.

"Tomasina was born on my Dad's birthday and named after the nickname he gave me.

"It has been very hard for us to put down our dogs when the time comes. One of the toughest was Bully Dog. We even cleared out our dining room at our house in Memphis, put plastic over the furniture and put a bed in there.

"We loved Bully Dog so much and Billy had a hard time letting him go. Greg, our security guard, was giving Bully morphine

"You have to have a sense of humor to tolerate me, and thankfully Tommie did."

shots to keep him alive. Finally one day, Billy knew he had to let Bully Dog go.

He got down on his hands and knees and told Bully, 'You're an old man and I'm even an older man. It's all right if you want to go home. I release you to go home. But before I die, I hope that God is good enough to me to give me another Bully Dog.' "

This is where I've been blessed all my life to have friends like Ronnie Grisanti. He remembers recognizing my grief over losing Bully:

"Billy still claims one of the greatest gifts he's gotten from anyone was a yellow lab named Atom Cat. That was my dog, and I gave it to Mr. Billy because I didn't have the room to work the dog

every day like you should. When I gave Atom Cat to Billy, Billy didn't have a dog at that time and he wasn't looking for one.

"I said, 'Billy, I want you to have this dog. His name is Atom Cat. I don't know whether you'll like him or not. He's a pretty good dog, but he still needs some work and he needs some ducks shot over his head.'

"From then on until the summer of 2014 when Billy had to put Atom Cat down – that was a very sad day – he and that dog had an unbelievable relationship. I've got pictures of Atom Cat lying next to Billy on Billy's bed.

"Every time I see Billy, he thanked me for giving him Atom Cat because Atom Cat brought so much joy to Billy. Every time Atom Cat had a birthday, Tommie would write me a note and remind me of the day I gave Atom Cat to him. Giving him Atom Cat sort of sealed our friendship with stronger concrete."

Now here's what we didn't know at the time when Ronnie gave me Atom Cat. It turns out Bully Dog was Atom Cat's uncle. You can't tell me that wasn't divine canine intervention.

Our love of dogs is one of the many interests I share with Tommie. It's nice that many of our friends and former employees recognize Tommie is a great fit for me:

Rev. John Sartelle, Billy and Tommie's minister: *"Tommie is the best thing to ever happen to Billy. She has loved him unconditionally from the beginning and she adapted.*

"Billy attacked business and he lived fast. He would get caught in his own world, but Tommie always had her own life.

"She's very confident. She was not intimidated by Billy's life and she fit into it. She could live fast, take care of him and retain her own identity. That's a rare individual that can do that under those circumstances.

"She dotes on him, cares for him. She's a real blessing for him."

Russ Cherry, Dunavant Enterprises attorney: *"Everybody that deals with Tommie realizes what a genuinely nice person she is. Anything you do for her or the Boss (Billy), she always sends handwritten thank-you notes. That's what she calls her 'ministry.' The notes are like therapy.*

"Tommie represents the soft side of the Boss, because it's something he just didn't do. She's like his public relations person. She can be a whirling dervish, talking 90 miles a minute. When she gets wound up, just step back.

"She's a very spiritual woman, a very Christian lady. She has that spirituality that's not bogus. Some people can talk the talk, but can't walk the walk. She walks the walk, but at the same time she's down-to-earth. She's not high society at all.

"The Boss and Tommie's daughter Kelli are the two objects in her life she focuses on. She gives everything she has taking care of the Boss. She's brought out all the Boss' good qualities.

"Tommie has had to deal with a blended family, because of the Boss' children from his first two marriages. Under some difficult circumstances sometimes, she has always maintained her grace.

"When she first married the Boss, she was trying to understand his business and his relationships with different people.

"She added a social element to his company by throwing these memorable theme parties. It was wonderful working here, it was like being in Camelot with all the different parties. It was her touch to lighten things up.

"They connect on so many levels. From the very beginning, she's never been shy to go with the Boss to the duck blind. She's gone pheasant hunting with him, fishing with him. She goes on the boat with him. She sets up his turkey blind for him and sits with him while he turkey hunts.

"Her love of the outdoors matches his, as do their love of dogs.

"Tommie is the love of his life, no doubt about it. He lights up around her. She has always been there for him. She's 'The Rock.' "

Dale Hall, CEO of Ducks Unlimited: *"Billy and Tommie make a great team. She is a very intelligent, loving woman who has the same passion for conservation as Billy does. She's a sweetheart, but no nonsense. She's like Billy in that sense."*

Karen Rhoads, former Dunavant Enterprises New York buyer/seller: *"When I first met Tommie, I just connected with her right away. She's very true. She wasn't phony about anything. She's a tough cookie, too, and I really value our friendship."*

"Tommie and I are very close in age. There was one party where we were sitting in the ladies room. Billy comes in and says, 'I'm looking all over the place for the two missing people and here you are sitting here talking. I should have known.'

"He'd have to separate us at parties sometimes, because we would talk too much and it would just make him angry."

Tina Butler, Tommie's sister: *"It's hard to put into words how remarkable my sister Tommie is, the influence she has had in my life and in the lives of others.*

"Tommie reminds me of the wholesome Christian woman in Proverbs 31:25-30 that is described as a woman 'clothed in strength and dignity; she can laugh at the days to come. She speaks with wisdom, and faithful instruction is on her tongue. She watches over the affairs of her household and does not eat from the bread of idleness . . . many woman do noble things, but you surpass them all. Charm is deceptive, and beauty is fleeting; but a woman who fears the Lord is to be praised.'

"My sister is all of those things; she is beautiful, hard working and wise. Above all else, she is one of the strongest Christian women that I know. She is actually the reason I am a Christian today.

"When I was younger, I remember Tommie coming home from college and talking to me about Jesus. I looked forward to her visits, because she was always encouraging me to grow spiritually.

"She also has the biggest heart for helping others. An example of her compassion is she constantly sends little notes to those in her life to let them know she is thinking about them. Her notes never fail to brighten my day.

"Tommie is more than a sister to me. She is my best friend. I am thankful for all she has done in my life and I love her so much."

Neely Mallory, lifelong Dickhead: *"Hands down, Tommie is the best thing that's ever happened to Billy. She has the temperament to handle Billy's impulsiveness when it comes to changing plans. He likes it when he verbally jabs Tommie and she jabs back. It takes that kind of give-and-take to have a happy marriage."*

Henry Morgan, lifelong Dickhead: *"Tommie is a very thoughtful and caring friend, as well as a great wife for Billy. She constantly writes notes to people, which I greatly respect."*

Chuck Smith, lifelong Dickhead: *"Billy and I were single about the same time after we each had gone through a couple of marriages. Sometimes during our noon tennis matches at The Racquet Club, we'd swap stories about some of the dates we'd go on and we'd laugh about it.*

"But when he started dating Tommie, it was interesting.

"On one of their early dates, Billy took Tommie to Coffeeville for bird hunting. She wasn't shooting, but her job was to pick up birds he shot. He shoots this bird, she goes out looking around and she can't find it.

"He said jokingly, 'It's just to your right, stupid." And Tommie proceeded to talk to him in a way nobody else dared to talk to him. I think he appreciated that.

"I know how Billy feels about her. He doesn't hide it. I saw him stand up in front of a crowd when he was being honored by Conservation Through Art and cry while saying, 'I love my wife.'

The Dunavants at home with three members of their "family."
"Among the many things Tommie and I share in common is our love of dogs."

"Tommie is very empathic and compassionate. She senses what he's feeling with his family. She has a total dedication to Billy. She is just perfect for him."

Jane Roberts, reporter from *The Commercial Appeal* in Memphis, who spent several days with the Dunavants at the Crazy D in Montana: *"Tommie is really aware of Billy's needs, very aware of him as a CEO who liked daily structure. Now I don't know that wasn't her way before she met him, because I could see her acting that way herself, being very precise about schedules, never being late, being very organized.*

"But she was smart to see how he operates and take that as her own. Because not being organized around Billy would create tension.

"They are very respectful of each other, and they try to help each other.

"When I was in Montana, he couldn't get the computer to work so he could watch the cotton exchange. It was a crisis. He was yelling, 'Tommmmmmiiiiieeeee.' She came in and figured out how to get the U.S. cotton exchange in Montana so he could be himself again.

"They both have this great regard for humanity. They'd take these long walks together in the morning in Montana, no matter the weather. They'd talk to the people along the way they met. They'd talk to anybody. It's very interesting they see the world that way.

"Billy loves jousting with people. Maybe a lot of people aren't comfortable enough to give it back to him.

"Have you ever seen Billy in a pair of shorts? When I was in Montana, he was going on and on about this duck on his property that liked him, that when he went outside that duck followed him around. I say, 'Billy, that duck doesn't like you. Look at your legs. That duck thinks you're his mother.'

John Stokes, lifelong Dickhead: *"Tommie keeps Billy going. She's not overbearing and she's totally devoted to him. She protects him. Billy just loves her and worships her. She has one of the kindest hearts. She brings a lot of gifts and writes a lot of notes to people. When we see her, she always brings some munchies for our dog Gus. She's a very devout Christian and so is Billy. They pray together and love God together."*

Ann Stokes: *"I think Tommie and Billy came into each other's lives at a time where they could devote a lot of time to each other. She's a very creative person with many ideas."*

Trow Gillespie, lifelong Dickhead: *"What strikes me first about Tommie and Billy's relationship is how much they have in common; their energy and enthusiasm, their passion, fervor and gusto for life, the spirituality they share with each other and their commitment to tackle just about any challenge together or individually. It is a relationship founded in consummate respect for each other.*

"Tommie is thoroughly and completely grounded in Billy, and knows him inside and out. Without question, she is his champion and advocate, and she certainly holds her own as a force to be reckoned with when it comes to Billy's well-being. Her pizzazz and spunkiness perfectly match her humility, which is one of her most endearing qualities.

"Like Billy, she is motivated and inspired by always having plenty of irons in the fire, constantly looking for ways to better our Memphis community. She is both a central and pivotal importance in Billy's life, and her devotion shows through in every facet of their relationship. If there is a predominant theme in Tommie's life, it is God first and Billy next.

"What a gracious lady!"

Coleman Connell: *"Tommie brings Billy 100 percent happiness and 100 percent support. She supports him like nobody has ever supported him."*

Tommie and I have our strengths and weaknesses that balance each other, which is we truly love each other and consider each other our best friend. It's why every time I hear Kenny Rogers' song "Through the Years," it perfectly reflects the way I feel about Tommie:

I can't remember when you weren't there,
When I didn't care for anyone but you,
I swear we've been through everything there is,

Can't imagine anything the two of us can't do.

Through the years,
You've never let me down,
You turned my life around,
The sweetest days I've found,
Through the years.
I've never been afraid,
I've loved the life we made,
And I'm so glad I've stayed,
Right here with you,
Through the years.

I can't remember what I used to do,
Who I trusted, whom I listened to before,
I swear you've taught me everything I know,
Can't imagine needing someone so,
But through the years it seems to me,
I need you more and more.

Through the years,
Through all the good and bad,
I knew how much we had,

I've always been so glad,
To be with you,
Through the years.
It's better every day,
You've kissed my tears away,
As long as it's okay,
I'll stay with you through the years.

Through the years,
When everything went wrong,
Together we were strong,
I know that I belonged,
Right here with you,
Through the years.
I never had a doubt,
We'd always work things out,
I've learned what love's about,
By loving you,
Through the years.

William Buchanan Dunavant Jr.
"Thanks for stopping by to read my story. I hope you learned a little something and maybe had a laugh or two."

15
Exhaling

"I'm not saying I'm through by any means,
'Cause there's still things that I want to say and do.
I hope you won't forget me, 'cause we shared a lot of dreams.
And just know I'll always remember you."

IT SEEMS AS THE OLDER I'VE GOTTEN, THE MORE George Strait songs like "I'll Always Remember You" speak clearly to me, especially after I finally retired.

Some of my children were pressuring me to retire from the time I was 60. I wasn't ready, so I didn't. They tried again when I turned 65 and then 70.

I had no reason to retire. It was my company and my money. I enjoyed what I did. I take off when I want to. I liked the boss — me.

I know from the outside I looked like a heavyweight boxing champion who didn't know when to quit.

But I needed to know if my children could handle the business. I had a very good friend in the textile business that died when he was 93 years old and he was still CEO. His son became CEO at the age of 74.

I would have hated if something suddenly happened to me, my sons were left running the business and they couldn't do it. So when I was 72, I finally concluded I needed to step back and see what they were able to do while I'm still alive.

I officially announced my retirement in New Orleans on January 5, 2005, at the Beltwide Cotton Conference where I always delivered an annual outlook speech.

I told everybody I would be done a few months later in June, though I would always be chairman of the board. Everything about the market was a little different. It was going in a high-tech direction and I wasn't educated in that direction. Maybe age mellowed my risk level.

It all made me feel a little uneasy as Russ Cherry, our Dunavant Enterprises attorney, remembers:

"The Boss said, 'I don't know how to trade the market anymore. It's not trading on fundamentals. The electronic trading and the way it's traded, if I can't trade with confidence, I don't need to be in it anymore.'

"That's when we started our negotiation early in 2009 with Allenberg, a subsidiary of Louis Dreyfuss based in France. It was an 18-month negotiation and Joe Nicosia was the CEO of Allenberg division.

"Joe was a man of his word. Lawyers dicker and negotiate over the terms. Whenever we hit a loggerhead, Joe and Billy would go in a room, BOOM, come out done. They always came to an agreement, shaking hands. They had been respectful opponents for 25 years, and now No. 1 was buying No. 2."

My main concern was making sure my employees were taken care of after the sale was completed in April 2010.

I was so involved in the cotton business, 24 hours a day. I was on call all the time, but it was okay. I thrived on it. It kept me alive.

But once I sold the cotton company, I have never, never looked back and said, "I made a mistake. I did the wrong thing." Nahhh. I've been happy every day. It was the right decision.

What made it easier was selling to a competitor that I respected, Joe Nicosia, who I tried to hire one time. Joe is a fine man and he recalls how the sale transpired:

"It was crazy. I'd never seen a transaction between the No. 1 and No. 2 cotton companies in the world done without a lawyer. It was done with mutual respect and trust, what's right, what's not.

"I'm sure Billy was getting people saying he needed to have corporate lawyers involved and I was getting that from my side. We just said, 'Stay out of it. Let's us do what's right.'

"In our business, it has to be that a man's word is his bond.

"I wasn't surprised that Billy sold it, because the world has changed. All the commodity businesses, the capital requirements are so huge now. The amount you have to put at risk is different.

"So I think he made the right decision when that time came up. It wasn't because he was unable, not because he couldn't compete, but because the stakes at the table were different than they were when he came through.

"I think it took a lot of courage to make that decision, because even today he knows he could still be successful in the business. He knows he could still carve out his ability to be profitable and run an enterprise.

"But it would come at a different risk and he'd have to risk his family, his time, his commitment. That was probably more than what he wanted to swallow at that time.

"I'm not surprised at his decision. I actually admire him for that decision. He would never have retired otherwise. It's in his blood, it's not his job, it's his life, it's his passion. I'm sure he still has it in his veins."

When I retired, I retired.

I know there are people who have known me well through the years, like my son Buck who's so like me, who wonder how I would suddenly adjust from such a breakneck pace all those years:

"Here I am . . . just call me Billy."
PHOTOGRAPH BY KAREN PULFER FOCHT / *THE COMMERCIAL APPEAL* / LANDOV

"I wish my Dad would have never retired. Retirement just is not for my Dad. He has a lot of hobbies, but I would have liked for him to keep trading cotton on a daily basis like his old friend Eli Tullis in New Orleans. Eli is still challenging his mind on a daily basis. You don't have to sit behind a desk to trade cotton."

Some of my Dickheads like Chuck Smith couldn't help asking me about the sale:

"On one of our duck hunts right after the sale was announced, I asked Billy about the difficulty of deciding to sell since his father started the company that had become such a fabric of Billy's life. I said, 'How did you arrive at the decision to sell it?'

"He looked at me very matter-of-factly and said, 'Our business plan didn't work anymore. We had no choice.'

"I'm sure Billy looked at every option possible before making the decision to sell."

I'm sure people have tried to figure me out during my career. The more successful I became, the more people sought my advice or wanted to know my secrets. What did I have that gave me an edge?

My old friend, the late Jim Daughdrill, who was president of Rhodes College in Memphis and a friend from my school days at McCallie, probably said it best a while back:

"What makes Billy Dunavant tick? I think I know some things.

"One is a sense of history. When I asked his office for a bio, it began, so characteristically, with the history of the cotton industry.

"His parents were an inspiration. I think he still hears his father. When the great jazz musician Hoagy Carmichael was told of the death of his friend and mentor Bix Biederbeck, Carmichael stopped, got a faraway look in his eye and said, 'That's funny. I can still hear him.

"Competition is a powerful motivator. What makes a man keep working who has all the money that he personally would spend for the rest of his life? I think a partial answer is a scoreboard – whether you keep score in sets or in dollars or in points or in ducks or in touchdowns or in jobs. Billy is a competitor.

"His faith makes him tick. His love of God is seen in his love of his fellow man.

He has a sense of beauty, he sees poetry where others may not, in getting to the heart of the matter, in being decisive, in simplicity. He is exhilarated by the beauty of excellence.

"And his family makes him tick."

Through the years, I've given hundreds, maybe even thousands of speeches. But probably the ones I have enjoyed the most are speaking to graduating classes, because I have philosophies that shaped my life.

And I guess right here, as I wind down this book, I want to pass them along to you.

It's important that you learn to appreciate your mother and father. I didn't realize that for many years after I got out of school, because I took them for granted and didn't appreciate the sacrifices they made for me.

I believe that you can't compromise your values, the values you learned at home, at church, even through your education. I saw many people in business who lowered their values and their futures were immediately put in jeopardy.

Goals are important. Short-term goals are better than long-term goals, for there is a greater measure of satisfaction and personal fulfillment when a goal is reached.

But as I learned, especially after reading Mitch Albom's book *Tuesdays with Morrie*, goals don't have to relate to personal success.

Goals can be something as simple as making a friend out of an enemy, making a contribution to the communities in which you live. I had to learn to become a giver, not a taker.

You have to learn to get along with people. Regardless of whether you are a farmer, lawyer, housewife or teacher, you will find in order to be a success you must get along with the world. You have to step outside of yourself and understand that you are not the only person with problems.

You have to be happy with yourself and your inner being. Just feeling this within yourself will automatically radiate to everyone around you.

A lot of my friends talk about my competitiveness, and I know I have been overcompetitive at times. But it kept me aggressive and it gave me the drive to give a second and third effort, because nothing of importance ever comes easily.

People have always said I got more out of my business day than the average person. The secret to that is something I learned as a teenager attending McCallie – time management.

So every day when I walked in my office, my mission was to complete every task for that day. I hated to go home with papers or letters unanswered. That didn't happen often because of my time management and organization skills.

Finally, I've constantly reminded myself that I could have not created and built what happened in my life and my family's life without God.

God gave me the opportunity to set the goals and meet the challenges. Nothing would have been possible without God as my leader. He is my greatest value.

It took me a long time to realize that it really wasn't me, it was Him. Personal success will only manifest itself when you comprehend you can't do it by yourself. Again, God is your leader.

Thanks for stopping by to read my story. Hope you learned a little something and had a laugh or two.

And if by chance we cross paths one day and you want to say hello, please, just call me Billy.

Take me home, George Strait:

"I knew the stakes right from the start,
When she dealt the cards I dealt my heart,
Now I just found a game that I can't play,
This is where the cowboy rides away.

"And my heart is sinking like the setting sun,
Setting on the things I wish I'd done,
Oh the last good-bye's the hardest one to say,
And this is where the cowboy rides away,
Oh the last good-bye's the hardest one to say,
And this is where the cowboy rides away."

"There's nothing better than enjoying life with old friends like Henry Morgan."

Acknowledgements

AS WRITERS ARE APT TO DO, WE ZIG WHEN we're supposed to zag, like I'm about to do, discussing who helped me finish this book instead of who got me in the front door to start it.

This project would not have been completed without the love and support of my wife Paige. She talked me down off the ledge several times and always had great ideas. No one sees the big picture and connects the dots better than Paige.

I'd also like to thank my dogs, the white fluffy Bichons Sophie, Gracie and Buddy. Sometimes when I was stuck staring at the computer searching for the right words, they made me take them for walks that cleared my cluttered head.

A nod to Marcus Carmouche and John Roach, my bosses at NOLA.com/*The Times-Picayune* newspaper in New Orleans where I'm a sports columnist. The support I received doing this project was unlike anything I've experienced in my 35-year professional career. It meant so much to me.

Thanks to the crew at Contemporary Media, Inc., in Memphis – publisher/CEO Kenneth Neill, business development director Jeffrey Goldberg, creative director Brian Groppe and editors Frank Murtaugh and Michael Finger – who efficiently brought this project home.

I would have never gotten a chance to co-author this book if my longtime friend Steve Ehrhart, executive director of the AutoZone Liberty Bowl, hadn't championed my cause. He probably thinks I owe him beers for life. He may be right.

Many thanks to Dunavant Enterprises attorney Russ Cherry and Becky Vega, Billy's administrative assistant. Russ provided valuable background information while Becky handled just about any request I made.

They both probably think I owe them free lunches for life. They also may be right.

A huge debt of gratitude to Billy's friends and former employees all over the world, and also to his sons. They all graciously gave me their time and their stories. This book improved with each one of their tales and remembrances.

Also, a big shoutout to the keen copyediting eye and contributions of Kelli Dunavant. Like your well-organized mother, you don't miss anything!

There are no adequate words to express how Billy and Tommie Dunavant opened their lives and their hearts to me.

Tommie is an absolute loving, caring dynamo. Her constant encouragement and reassurance every time we talked gave me the good vibe to keep on keeping on.

Finally, there's Billy, whom I had known professionally through his Memphis athletic ownership endeavors when I was writing for *The Commercial Appeal.*

I was initially hesitant to pursue this project. Because when you start researching Billy's career, there are so many layers it's overwhelming. His business accomplishments are staggering. His philanthropy is overwhelming – he's given away more money than I could make in 50 million lifetimes.

But once I dug into this book, I quickly realized he might be one of the most unpretentious people I've ever met. Billy prefers blue jeans and a good steak over a tux and "pretty" food.

He's a guy's guy.

As this book progressed, I discovered what drove him to the top of the world cotton business for decades and decades.

It was never about the money he made, the wealth he acquired.

It was the daily scoreboard. At the end of each day, did he win the market?

If he did, he was giddy because Billy loved to win. But he was also gracious, because he knew he might lose his butt the next day. Nobody turned a page faster, win or lose, than Billy.

I'm grateful and proud Billy chose me to help him tell his story.

I'm humbled that now when we haven't seen each other for awhile, Billy greets me with, "Higgins, you Dickhead, what have you been doing?" In keeping with Billy's love of country singer George Strait, these are lyrics from George's song "The Road Less Traveled" that will always remind me of Billy:

And there's a road, a winding road that never ends,
Full of curves, lessons learned at every bend,
Goin's rough unlike the straight and narrow.

It's for those who go against the grain,
Have no fear, dare to dream of a change,
Live to march to the beat of a different drummer,
And it all might come together,
And it all might come unraveled,
On the road less traveled.

For the road less traveled ain't for the faint of heart,
For those who choose to play it safe and never stray too far,
Me I wanna live my life and one day leave my mark,
And it all might come together,
And it all might come unraveled,
On the road less traveled.

I've chosen a pathway I may not endure,
One thing's for certain nothin's for sure,
And it all might come together,
Or it all might come unraveled,
On the road less traveled,

Chief Dickhead, you're the best!

Ron Higgins, July 2015